EARLY WRITING

Frank O'Hara

EARLY WRITING

Edited by Donald Allen

Grey Fox Press
Bolinas, California

Cover photograph: taken in 1950 by George Montgomery

Library of Congress Cataloging in Publication Data

O'Hara, Frank.
   Early writing.

   Includes index.
   I. Title.
PS3529.H28E3   811' .5'4   77-652
ISBN 0-912516-16-X
ISBN 0-912516-17-8 pbk.

The publication of this volume was partially supported by a grant from the National Endowment for the Arts, Washington, D.C., a federal agency.

Grey Fox Press books are distributed by Book People, 2940 Seventh Street, Berkeley, California 94710.

CONTENTS

EDITOR'S NOTE

This volume collects Frank O'Hara's writing during the years he was a student at Harvard College: the earliest poem is dated October 1946 and the latest August 1950. All dates given in brackets following the poems are from the poet's manuscripts; undated poems are placed where any evidence suggests they belong.

The first group of poems comes from a brown leather looseleaf notebook. Apparently in the late summer of 1949, O'Hara typed up on punched notebook paper most of the shorter verse he had written during the preceding three years, meticulously dating each poem, and then destroyed the original drafts. Several of these poems also exist as separate manuscripts: perhaps they were typed out for courses.

The poems in the second section come from manuscripts in O'Hara's papers dating from the same period, plus a handful of more achieved poems from his last year at Harvard. Together with the Notebook Poems, they provide an exceptional opportunity to study the poet's progress: from early rehearsals of traditional forms and themes through experimental and prose poems and verse portraits of friends to the "psychological and autobiographical" poems (to coin a phrase) for which he was first best known. (The reader will also wish to consider with the poems in this volume those published in the first twenty pages of *The Collected Poems* [Knopf, 1971].)

A third section presents the only Journal O'Hara appears to have kept, plus a fascinating account of his wartime experiences, "Lament and Chastisement" (written for Professor Albert Guérard, who gave it a B+), and other papers presumably written for courses.

I am most grateful to Maureen Granville-Smith for making her late brother's papers available to me: the editing of this volume and of *Poems Retrieved* would not have been possible without close study of the manuscripts. I am also grateful to the following for warmly appreciated assistance: John Ashbery, Zoe Brown, John Ciardi, Margaret Cooley, Mary E. Cooley (Secretary, The Hopwood Room, University of Michigan Library), Kenneth Koch, Duncan Mac-Naughton, Lawrence Osgood, William Turner, Ben Weber and George Yeoman.

Donald Allen
January 2, 1977

NOTEBOOK POEMS
1946-1949

DIALOGUE FOR MAN, WOMAN & CHORUS OF FROGS

mary: I sigh, my dear
for the kinetic wishfulness
of stale eunuch's dung.
The end is practically a diddlebutt
and I refuse, absolutely, to prostitute my art
because you lack toothpaste.

george: Frog's frog you, and the will is done.
Ass for the pedestrian.
And still crickets glow
for the renascence of the kiss-form
in the afterglow.

mary: You mean as the fascine fluctuating
orgases me.
Fuck's fuck me
and the end in the run.
"Still crickets" for the final
of the bullrush foliated.
I sat, forzando.
And william's lips, fructose
pursed levulously:
I fructiferous, he frugiverous.
(For that matter
dishu, dowto, ducho.)

george: Bombast!
The reek of dried semen for the olfactory womb.
Die in the grass of the lamb!
Kiss the foot of the papal chamberpot
lest the gate to peter be locked against thee.
The halakah prescribes the ass,
the issue of the men of Babylon
drowns the Children of Light.
O mal de mer!

I am constipated by a lush red rose
and two flutes. Compris?

mary: Incaminate to defecate!
"Virtue is like precious odours, —
most fragrant when they are incensed and crushed."
Forgell non mein
the vista virva vanishes
as the speckled milky trout.
Ah! nacht und sprechstimme!

chorus: Give it to 'er, geo!

george: In nomine, papyrus.
Ab altare dei.
Hocus in hodiē. Pocus in anus.
Goosed, by god, goosed
by the god damned gorer of the gemsbok!
Do you think she's a homozygote?

chorus: Not piece, but the sword!
Ass for a razor blade?

george: Flog not thy zincy zither
in the crystalline starshine.
Phosphoresce my fingernail, mary,
my limp lump;
kiss my chuckle
as the nimbus numbly nuzzles.
Phartez-vous?

mary: I glug you glove.
Glave me your glabrous glans.

chorus: Giselle, my dear!
autumn has come, my tumtum.
For what? and the felled screw
ate his way home sadly,

for the prostation is poorly heated
and it is impossible
to get a pillow into a urinal,
much less a hot box.

mary &
george: Shit.

[November 15, 1946]

THE HIGHWAY

as cool as rushes
rush is
along the paved
as my dripping
anoints tar
coursing macadam
and the concrete
slipping
under my blood
o empty heart

[October 13, 1946]

SOLSTICE

The waning star
falls wanly to
the planets are
no vivid hue

but deftly looms
the creeping pink
the sun assumes
at the moonsink.

Stars nod without
they show their light
glimmer about
keep dark the night;

contrast is doom:
their function is
to tell the gloom
the night is his.

[January 25, 1947]

THE MILITARISTS

They never come
who always rise
and in the sun
they have pink eyes;
one never knows
just what they hope:

between their toes
they carry soap.

How do they know
when to grow?
Do they sense
when to fence?
How do they feel
about the wheel?
Have they aplomb
before they bomb?

When they march
do they never parch?
When they eat
do they move their feet?
Have they no terror
of being in error?
Have they forgot
what they made rot?

The end is just
for we are blind;
there's left to us
a lonely rind
and only the hazardous
dare guess
if they will spare us
when we've less.

[February 15, 1947]

7

AUGUST

Georgian fonts are old
their decor gold rococo smiles.

All gilts express coy grins
of fishes' fins on coloured tiles.

Ferocious men had seeped
as women weeped through wetted sod.

Gay courtiers now replace
in flirting grace the lust of virile bawd.

Warm women wander sad
look to be had by any hand.

Fetish is sign of this dear day
a fresco may contain a land.

[March 26, 1947]

RUNE

Out on the meadow hoed
five fliers
piled cut grassroots
in a load.

Out to the garden strode
five sailors
squashed frail violets
in their road.

Out of the gateway rode
five soldiers
held killed peacocks
left a toad.

[March 27, 1947]

HELLSHAFT

(*to George Barker*)

Really, said the red-faced axe-layer
you have such lovely hair.
Janus, said the red-faced axe-layer
your skin is so fair.

Really, said the red-faced axe-layer
you have flanks like a mare.
Janus, said the red-faced axe-layer
even clothed you look so bare.

Really, said the red-faced axe-layer
I just can't help but care.
Janus, said the red-faced axe-layer
we'd make a handsome pair.

Really, said the red-faced axe-layer
I desire you in my lair.
Janus, said the red-faced axe-layer
I'm jealous of the very air.

Really, said the red-faced axe-layer
a love like mine is rare.
Janus, said the red-faced axe-layer
let me; do you dare?

Really, said Janus, nibbling his ear
I'm not even here!

[April 2, 1947]

BLUES SONG

Piled creels
contain
the spinning.

Oh the fix we're in, the fix we're in.

Like heaped fences
creels climb
up around.

Oh the fix we're in, the fix we're in.

Without them we'd go off our bobbins,
Without them we'd go off our bobbins.

Oh the fix we're in, the fix we're in.

[April 4, 1947]

NACHTSTÜCK

Embossed with giant clams
the grave lagoon; the yams
salute a moon of dire
and god-impassioned ire.

Rococo streams of lit
moon-glint coral knit
in hint of shark-humps
guard a corpse in garish lumps.

Underneath the negro lies
love caught in liquid ties
in wrought seminal kiss
more permanent than bliss.

[April 5, 1947]

QUINTET FOR QUASIMODO

1

H. P. Leek: Morgan has only four legs, you know,
hardly a recommendation;
the dregs of society are, moreover,
largely inflated in bilious gradation.

2

Hannah: Fat people are almost invariably funny;
the sunny view of every ghastly scene
is partially desired from motives of self-
protection, i.e., delight in the obscene.

3

Roger: Gordian knots are somewhat umbilical:
have you ever seen a filial relationship
free from the rigours of pale devotion?
Sue: The urinary aspect of parturition falls, a-drip,

4

through practically every cheesecloth
mustard mastered lecherous bilge-pot.
Together: Naturally one assumes a rather careful broth
from such a mixture, perhaps we ought . . .

Coda

but just one other thing, if you're a Jew
give in to everybody's whims and fears. You
                                    are few.

[April 13, 1947]

MERDE

Jardin
jardin sous la plu-
ie   .Sous.

O, et moi, jardin? et moi?

Me remettez-vous?
Me remerciez-vous?

Je souffre.

[April 22, 1947]

L'ENNUI

Puisque, lorsque
aujourd'hui.
Je reviens à toi
et puis

notre pain quotidien
de l'angoisse s'efface.
Quelle mélasse.

[April 24, 1947]

SONG

If you were Miraflor
would you attend the garden gate,
would you stay by the door,
would you, foregoing pleasure, wait?

Miraflor is all dew:
she quickens, glistening, at his call.
She hopes they will be two;
he never comes to her at all.

[April 26, 1947]

LE COEUR SUR LA MAIN

Le pourchasseur est un garçon poupin.
Elle s'élance à travers le rassemblement,
l'enfant trouvé perpetuel. Enfin
mon mignon découvrit un recoin, attardement,

pour jeter le mouchoir à quelqu'un. Maintenant
vite mon fichu fait des préparatifs
pour une rencontre aux apéritifs.
Et donc? je ne sais pas, mon bébé, tellement.

[April 26, 1947]

PORTRAIT OF ALEXANDRA DANILOVA

Pale flame of flashing ice
the warmth of dashing spice
elucidates the torture
of the notes in posture

of an entity complete within
itself. The rhythm herein
portrays the casual carnage
of a sere motive montage

imposed upon the moving glacier
of the sound, the grim erasure
of the overbearing visual
failing to make the motion dismal.

14

It would seem
that your frail beauty
bears the only duty
toward the dream.

[April 26, 1947]

HOMAGE TO JOHN WEBSTER

If your mind has had enough of torture
you may like perhaps to change your posture:
bend yourself with harnesses of chains
or lay yourself upon nail-studded frames.

If you're the kind that takes alternatives
you may like to try the cure life gives:
drown your angst in sleek black fluid cars
or snuff it out between cold cream and stairs.

But if you've the guts avoid the ruts:
answer your fears with an end to years
finish the weep with a ceaseless sleep
stop the song that's been sung too long.

[April 29, 1947]

DAWN

Clustered it sways, damage-fettered,
dire dainty prism of evil.
There in the half-light,

flustered by the wind-waved sway of
wire-stalked grass, the snake-spit slides from
where it gathered through the night.

[May 1, 1947]

VIRTÚ

Marble niches frame a virgin's grey decay
as casually as rain clouds fill the day
with not quite black foreboding. As the sun
beams sickly on the desecrated fun
of cold lubricious shepherd boys
whose sheep are more to them than toys
a chalky white encases all but veins
of these dead innocents who washed by rains
retain a purity both circumspect and bold
that flaunts itself in pride of being old
and moans a bleak blear sermon to the crowd
which ignorantly adulates their pose in proud
and dumb misunderstanding of their deed:
it follows them self-righteously although they lead
to catacombs of filthy falsely thought of ways
which only add a burden to the price it pays.

[May 1, 1947]

DAS LIED FÜR DER ERWACHEND

Das Morgen frisst der Jungsein
mit feinem Grausamkeit,
mit feinem Gehorsamkeit.

Der Gott wandelt sich um unbestimmtlich
und Er kümmert sich schläfliglich;
was für ein Gott ebenso betragt sich?

Die Sonne, die das Morgen erhebend ist,
fühlt die Dienenruhe.

[May 19, 194

PORTRAIT OF JEAN MARAIS

Coursing blood is all the flood
the heart espies and then decries
as flowing in the winter night
it searches for a spring surmise.

Lavish in the heat the naked feet
splay bold against the cold
and hope they journey from their own
to more upon the barren wold.

Eighteen toes are all that's left
and curving arches scream bereft
wrinkles map a darkling chart
beneath the blowing bush.

17

Distance spreads away and far
the space behind a tingling star
the solstice aches and later quakes
to know the rue of what we do.

And when the pup at last gives up
the failing neck proclaims the wreck
the aged turn and try to learn
the dreary rote of what they tote.

[May 27, 1947]

HAVE YOU MET THE PRESIDENT OF THE GARDEN CLUB?

The mystic violet and encroaching ivy
are not so strange as those
who come and sniff a rose
and sip a cocktail; then are on their way.

A sinister and vicious pose is this:
who dares feign casualness to flowers
breaks old laws, offends large gods,
and casts a shadow forward on abyss.

The violet sweetly trips him,
the ivy checks his falling,
he swings like a ripe plum on a limb
until a tendril, breaking, stops his calling.

[May 31, 1947]

GAVOTTE

Alack alack alay
my ministrante has come to me
to lead the dark away.

Meetly she
embraces me
coolly drily tenderly.

In dawning air
her flesh grows fair
she feathers me with whispering hair.

The pinkness of
her breasts' warm dove
recalls the tumult of our hidden love.

As she lies
her water-eyes
steam in memory of darkness-covered sighs.

As morning grows
she the rose
blooms on my stem and on us sun-dust snows.

Alack alack alay
my last-night's love has come to me
to celebrate the day.

[August 11, 1947]

TORCH SONG

The brazen and the blameless
bear the brunt;
the shaven and the shameless
share the shunt;

what to do? what to do?
we never know WHAT to do.

[August 13, 1947]

MR. AUDEN IN LOVE: TWICE

1

You
the wise one and the warm   I know
have graced the temple
                    of too many tortures.

When
in the positions of our circumferic passion
you press for prize
                    I pray you dead;

while
I watch you wait for advantage over me
my heart speaks
                    and alone hears its hurt.

Why
if we deserve our lips' and laps' deliverance
must I bemoan
and you bemuse the beast?

2
You
who have seized me in your silence
as the desert wind's desire
inflames the dune

when
simoon's simmer arouses its sands
to heat that special hades:
if you hear

while
you stand still beneath the bulb's electric stain
the fine-grained undulation
of my love's ululant unbitting

why
do you remain so reticent of rapine
even though my blood
is blaring to share yours with you?

[August 12 & 16, 1947]

21

TRIOLET

The iron look in the frame of glass
    murdered the loose love in my face,
its blows exposed the mollient brass:
the iron look in the frame of glass
judged me weak, emotion crass;
    the whole affair was my disgrace.

The iron look in the frame of glass
    murdered the loose love in my face.

[August 31, 1947]

AGAPANTHUS

My own dear lord, my lord, she said
    the light is dim
    in our soft home
    and yet you nightly roam
    according to your whim
which leaves me restless by your bed.

I have compounded, lord, a paint
    of perfumed tiger's milk
    and smoky indigo
    which lends a glow
    like puddled silk
to all the flesh I choose to taint.

I have procured, my lord, a cloth
    of blinding golden sheen
    yet downy to the stroke

with hopes I should provoke
your negligent demean
to heat the hidden whiteness into froth.

I have arranged, my lord, my hair
to spiral highly soft
into a tender tower
and affixed a flower
sending scent aloft
to thus enhance, my lord, my fertile lair.

But you, my lord, affect to hear me not
and I in my distraction
no longer fight to save
love from the slave
and his brute action
careless if you should find us on his cot.

[September 3, 1947]

THE FATTENING NYMPH

When when o lord
she cried, the bawd
who on a silken pillow
sipped her coffee
tongued a toffee
as a willow sighed.

Ennui forever dear
she wailed at bier
of yellow roses
gritted ivory teeth

replaced the wreath
on her reposes nailed.

Tra la la
ah toodle;
kissed her poodle
tra la la.

[September 25, 1947]

FRESH AIR IS SO GOOD FOR YOU

The pale girl lies
on the green park bench
fighting the fringe of her eyes
that attempts a violet quench.

Slick oilcloth leaves
hold back her leaving sweat
press succour from her heaves
as the air inside grows wet.

Nodding blue hollyhocks
complacently ogle the trees
and never fret at writhing locks
as tentacles suck her lees.

[September 27, 1947]

JOURNAL DE MON AUTRE ANGOISSE

Dearie dearie me
mother is out to tea;
father's the lover
of mother's brother:
what is there left for me?

[September 27, 1947]

LA POUSSIÈRE D'UNE FLEUR PRÉCIEUSE

Heart-shorn, lip-sick, breath-weary
the Count assayed gavotte;
later while pavaning bit
his tongue to hide the rot.

Virile business for
a vicious man he thought
and hid beneath his cuff
the spot he wounded sought.

The pink and fluff danced by
with brilliant stabbing eyes;
toward the knife he rushed
to meet her little cries.

[October 3, 1947]

ABER, BLANCA

Your frenzied friend has left his mark:
the pot of purple paint has spilled,
it covers your pain-browned tapestry.
What will Sophia do now, poor thing?
(What can you do with flaming hair?)

That boy has not forgot the church
and you cannot forget for now that
Die Sevenste Bliscap van Maria
bleeds you new each year. (What care
you indeed? Who have yet years to go.)

Ännchen has taken to kissing dogs
for diversion; and I play Schönberg
with only a slight nervousness: it is
my home, my refuge from you all.
(And even if you are all here with me?)

The rain may never stop and you
may stay to play your Solo here.
Let the bitch wait for you have
her at your terms, as we all know.
(How long since you were in the Münster?)

You are so white and so terrible, hot
with truth, zealous with anguish; but you do
and ash-faced at that declare your holy
wards. Blanca: have you removed the cowl?
(And do you not yourself need change of air?)

[October 15, 1947]

DIRGE

Strophe

Seven salvages kissed the dust.
Dust has a pleasing flavor.
Anything tastes good if you're used to it.
Marian Bipple stayed stitching till the date of her death.
A girl can live if she doesn't try too hard.
Dust is someone's saddened bones.
Seven salvages kissed Marian's pelvis.

Antistrophe

A girl can keep her bones whether she wants to or not.
It was immodest.
Pink bones protest.
There are some people who only blush during adolescence.
A girl outgrows everything unless she wants to.
Embarrassment yields blood.
There are people who find blood nourishing.

Epode

May we not pray for Marian?
Better to weep.
I feel so useless.
They also weep who wail, and also spit who sob.
Utility is defunct.
Mucus has been the deliberate death of a great many people.
You can drown in anything if you try hard enough.

Strophe

Moisture insinuated Marian's decay.
There is a reason for sun worship.
No one tells what he knows.
There is a reason for everything if you know enough people.
There are seven books watching everyone.
Ink dries quickly.
Leaves contain life's secrets.

Antistrophe

Decay is a trinity.
Heat wets what binds.
The sun disappears too soon.
The cloud is not momentary, not astral, not conventional.
Mud pies address the sunshine.
A girl sees slime in a brick.
Circle, cycle, what have you.

Epode

Bipple is a maiden name.
Marian says may not have been a virgin.
Rain fertilizes the brick.
The danger is in death, but the worry is in wet.
A brick in a soup plate may crumble.
Marian Bipple was a beautiful brick.
Seven bricks build an outhouse.

Strophe

Love limps after a coffin.
A bone contains nostalgia.
Tears seem dust cement.
I have lamented Marian's decay.
Wet makes bricks make mud.
An outhouse is no monument.
Seven kisses seal a nothing.

The chorus is tired, I am tired.

[December 16, 1947]

OH PULCINELLA!

The wake is weaving tassels
for your hair and elbows, darling;
the horse and rider thrashing the surf
curry your curls in happiness.

The tilted soup plate in the sky
is spilling love-light on the waves
but I am moving away from you
though you cry aloud on the dock.

I wish someone would break the foghorn
before it breaks my heart;
on and on it sobs and remembers
your moaning love by the sea.

Wait for me, wait for me on the dock:
the sea may freeze over in winter
and I'll come skating back
like the great golden bird of paradise.

Oh Bruegel, you alone understand:
I feel like a shell that is broken,
my legs stick out to be stepped on
by a burgher with brain steeped in lust.

The size of the sea is keeping me here
though wintry winds are blowing,
and even if the water froze
I would have to learn how to skate.

[January 7, 1948]

POEM

Speeding autos chasing garters
track the street in falling snow.
Lacing bits of blood and martyrs
on the slippery highway's glow.

Headlights flicker at the smudges
scattered on the streaming floor,
shudder, but the walker budges
never, though on death's white shore.

Waiting for a streetcar Sally
shifts her parcels in her arms,
Enid begs her not to dally
lest an auto bruise her charms;

Sally loiters, then too late
races for her rumbling tram,
Enid screams at skidding fate
as Sally feels a gentle slam.

Snow-way pinked by lethal tires
now is pinked with Sally's blood,
and, while Sally's life expires,
Sally's garters soak in mud.

Netted loosely in the night
snow is held by motorcars;
one runs on with broken headlight
winking at unwinking stars.

[January 17, 1948?]

IMAGE

Mice green as grass
lope
thunder
shaded sidewalks
mouseturds ricochet
ping: plate-glass window
poop: concrete block
ploop: pavement
piddle: down the street.

Scraping claws dig ditches
while the dawn demurs.

Mice grey as gangrene
scurry
scamper
fading shadows
hasten to holes
seek damp dark
rust tin cans
garbage puddles
cesspools: sanctuary.

Sun! Death lust pursues
but whose?

[January 20, 1948]

MACARONIC

Racing, mincing mice
    Allons, mes drôles,
devour the dropping rice
   before it floors and bounces.
     chantez sans paroles!
The scrambling leader jounces,
biting heads and limbs.
    Chantez sans sourire,
They roll and squeak on whims
  and, finishing the food,
    chantez de mourir!
go home to eat their brood.

                    [January 20, 1948]

FOR NATASHA

My darling let us listen
to the horses' hooves that beg
our silence and the tears that glisten
in the ash-castrated cigarette end's glow.

What's welled up within us
may be the ages that have died
and spills out such rusty pus
to wash the worn and bloody pedes.

The march has been long
and we always unmounted
have fallen together from the strong
to waste of thirst in this dried-up stream.

The accident happened so quick
that it was fatal to us both;
till my saliva's dry I'll lick
your throat, but my tongue is already limp.

We should have stumbled past
oh my dear this oasis
where now our love is so bound fast
that it may only flatter earth's fertility.

[February 20, 1948]

QUATRAIN

Lilac lady peers at day
under rick of hennaed hay
then assembles her visage
with a blast of maquillage.

[February 28, 1948]

BEACON HILL

The houses are ghettoes of ghouls
and out in the stagnant pools
the heads of maidens
deflowered on whim
decompose
and rise to the rim.

[March 1, 1948]

BALLAD

Lorna Doone once met my aunt
and they rode off together;
your lovely head, said Lorna Doone,
should be encased with leather,

and off she pulled a Russian boot.
The two rushed on through night and rain,
the lovely head began to pain,
why did it have to be such awful weather?

[March 2, 1948]

SONG

Deny deny
the green flushed poppy
and the reeling sense
smoked in the house
of orient incense.

While in dark
groping the spidered corridor
toward the drunk lust
steaming in the room
hung with rust

deny deny
the stench of poppies
burnt to stain your love
a brown manure
so you can drop it, lover

don't deny.

[April 9, 1948]

SONG

Where kiss-killed queans
and lotus-ravished virgins
lie
within beige pyramids
of Nefertiti's teats a
memory,
camels hawk their spit
of onion phlegm and
die
beside the gaping dunes
that shifting swallow all.

The palace on the delta Nile
is ruled now by a crocodile;

on dusty marble floors is dung;
songs are croaked now, never sung.

Pale-buttocked dancing boys
and wraith-ribbed maidens now
parade
in burning breezeless sun
and beg from fetid sweating
clay
on garbage littered streets
a little rotting rice as
aid.

Their drying corpses smell as
sweet and velvet as a pall.

[April 9, 1948]

DECLINE & FALL

Over the Jews the eagle squatted
    hatching hate
and on their bodies squalid
    sweat-slimed, sores

like blood-money, festered;
    pus, in globules
blistered fatly, fell ripe
    with disease.

Rome, in final majesty, struck
    casting bait
of contagion into streams
    and shores

crowded with watching lust
    that milled in pools
surged, and flooded, by the loin
    of the beast.

                                        [April 16, 1948]

STILL LIFE

Slipping into the sentry's hut
(the door stood wide
and in the sun
how dried
the blossom grows
that has not died

to let the womb
bloom)
the worm glides
pushing
into the inner room
eating
the walls and floors
(the gnat explores
hushing
no vague heart
beating
no pale wings
hearing
no murmurs of light sounds refraining
seeing
no soft shadows
echoing
through charted chambers
remembered passages
fearing
no pitch no pressure no collapse)
searching
there in the fragile chest
hidden beneath the floor
finding
the single seed
grinding
with indifferent muscle
the fructive core
browning the blood
(so small the germ
so frail the sperm
so dead the need)
of the seed.

[May 7, 1948]

SUITE FOR MILITARY BAND

1 Gavotte

When I met Beulah
in Chicago
(o Beulah
in Chicago)
by the shores
of Michigan Lake,
on the shingle
we would tingle
in fits of bliss
we'd long to kiss
(but we wouldn't
for Beulah's sake);
the sea was slurping
on the sand
I was burping
behind my hand
between us two
(sad day) we threw
into
the lake
(o sad mistake)
our fit of bliss
our long to kiss
and drowned them both
(for Beulah's sake).

2 Waltz

When we're
       gliding a-
       long on the
       back of a
       mare at the

fair-grounds
it's heaven!

Oh it's

nice to be
tight on a
night when the
moon filters
down on the
crown of your
panama
hat!

See the

music re-
sounds as the
hobby horse
bounds we'll be
seasick
together!

And I'll

take you right
home if you'll
kiss me and
promise to
loan me the
trolley car
fare!

3 Habanera

Oh, light darkens
the dark stir opens
a vault of blue-air
and dead-green leaves.

See: wraiths rise-now
in dead-green wrappers
their shrouds of sea-moist
moss velveteen,

and, their voices
like souls of oysters
of dark blue pansies
serenade.

4 Rhumba a la Jazz

Black satin chassis
(You're an oldsmobile!)
with a blossom at your valley
and the (Boom! boom!) drums of Seville
at your back,
there's a dark dark alley
just outside the next drink
where the (Reet! teet!) steep deep blue
begins!

"Albert! Albert!
"Let go of my skirt!
"Herman! Herman!
"You're unbuttoning your shirt!
"You'd better let go of me
"or you'll get hurt
"by my red (Hot!) lacquered fingernails!"

41

"Honey, lovey, when the boom starts in
"and the (Reet!) beat of the drum
"is talkin' of sin
"there's somethin' doin'
"in every dark place
"and if you holler you'll find
"a towel stuffed in your face!"

Your patent leather hair
(Hey! Guadeloupe!)
is sliding down
in a mesh on your nape
as the rearing trombones glare
and frown
and the writhing trumpets blare
around
and the smoke puffs up
(Bijou! Bijou!)
from the (Red hot!) hard hit
stiff stretched
hide bound drum
at your (Boom! boom!) back!

[May 7, 15 & 21, 1948]

POEM

Neon snakes mince
touching eyes and asses
in the rain; quince
scents counterpoint them

as a lady passes
with a swinging hem;

they spin slowly while
the buffer of the night
rubs their blossoms bright,
they ignite
at the hand of the acolyte
in tiers of tears,
incense of quince,
along the dark wet aisle.

[May 21, 1948]

SONG

Grim is the water
of my true love's hair
and steel grey the color
of her hirsute sea.

Mauve are her breasts:
they have tarnished tassels,
the tinsel of their hairs
lattices her ribs.

She smiles and the dawn
tingles an answer,
the song of her laugh
lightens the dark

and the sun, a lech
of grease colored fire,
grins the day's lust
in a dew-dying grimace.

[May 21, 1948]

43

DECADENCE

When the whisper is silent
and the elegant heart is jet
the world can't find a talent
to say, "The weather's wet";

to say, "there's trouble, trouble—
and I'm sicker than I seem";
the unuttered world's too feeble
when the well-lit heart's agleam.

[October 11, 1948]

A MADRIGAL

Collecting idle tears in buckets
limp as shrouds we played
with our thin and commonplace fears
like uneasy kings with crowds;
we summoned regents of love and rosary,
ate larger meals and gulped down pills,
ironed out wills with steam jets and
to pay for mistakes saw a masseur:
but somewhere in the Turkish mists
we found ourselves becoming toys
and braced our feet against the spongy walls
so not to lose our baby sovereignty.

[August 3, 1949]

OTHER POEMS
1946-1950

[WHITE AND CASUAL, HOW THE BREATH]

White and casual, how the breath
   drifts out of body into the air
of winter as if body's pith
   were spitting slowly, without care

for passer-by; but purposeful
   as the fetid damp bed-sitting rooms
that push out queasy odors, fill
   the sun-cleaned street with linty brooms.

Drifts? Deliberate as a sketch
   or graph of wickedness whose ease
is sly and pretty! There's a catch:
   the wind's no fiercer strangling trees

than breath when round a neck it slips.
   Easily, at random, fish are scathed
in just this way by cast-out slops,
   and bloated where they clear had bathed.

PORTRAIT OF JAMES JOYCE

riverrun,said jute,oh why the enterrential
faggus?
discolum in ionic,doric or sabbatic
juicecum?
which wherewithal you never can
to bother with the endspin of a dustweb
for the categoric is a tombstone,—
dingy,discrete,and rancidulous.

frost my nuts if it isnt the saint!
bon giorno,aloysius,my feathermusking friend!
draw up a syllogism to rest your fatass on.
the birth of the blues is on today
and as a special intermission feature
we have an exhibition of syncopated menstruation.
interested? knew you would be,you old bastard,you.
pushaw,man,scratch not thy palm,as it says in genesodus,
lest the seeds of masturchism be sown therein.
cant beat the goodbook,can you?
jesus i thought id come in my pants reading about oompha.
but to get back to the subject,
forbisnits thy furgumbang?
disnits?
just what i told the old lady and she said i had the clap.
funny world,eh? unh? ummmmmmmmmmmmm.salty...
that teresa mustave been a good one.
spiritual quality,you say?
recited rimbaud while you ate—oyes i get indigestion too.
of course youre not abnormal,al.

a bit of the socratic nymphus mixed with the phrygian phallus
is all and not a goddamn thing wrong with it.
adds spice id say.
what?
not dithyrambic but rather tocuscular.
the mixolydian anapest has a definitely libidinous connotation.
purge it.yes.purge.
such a flowerous floaping flabber.
like the thick ooze of diarrheal defecation.
kill them all for all i give a shit.
havent lived long enough to know what theyve missed.
let it float in the gutters.remind people to go to church.
does em good.little blood never hurt anybody.
except a virgin—thought youd like that one,al.
oh sure.well shake it easy.bon giorno.

and then the ferrulatus fell
crushing the mass of titblooms
so soft salacious
caress
and i cried.hours.not wept.
cried.
like liffey.
and im just a stone.
i lost it all you see.
now i just watch riverrs,
and wish it was me.

[November 25, 1946]

HAVE YOU EVER?

Morning mist is quite the wildest thing; I hardly have the courage to face it. It's getting so I hate to stay up late; I just never go to cocktail parties any more because I'm afraid I'll get tight and find myself still up at dawn. Jesus, it's frightening. Do you know what it's like to feel yourself being slowly and gradually absorbed in a mild mist? You have no idea. It can only happen to you once, and then you spend the rest of your life avoiding it. It's never quite so bad after that. You are so frightened by it all—you just wait. And anything that comes can't quite measure up to your fear. In a way it's a kind of insurance. Unless you think it is; if you do, of course, it loses all its value and you're lost. The vilest thing is to think you're immune. Never, never, think nothing can be worse than what you're at. It can, oh god, how can it. Well, you'll see, my dear. It's quite inevitable. It's happened to several of my friends already. Like the Black Plague you just never know where it will strike next. I'm glad I'm out of it now. You'd be amazed at how amusing it is to watch others suffer as you know you've already suffered,—and survived, of course, that's essential. Because you never know whether they will or not. Such a nice element of suspense. Of course, you wouldn't appreciate that, would you?

[April 13, 1947]

PORTRAIT OF J CHARLES KIEFE

Bright to the sun it came galloping up one morning dazzling
dizzling spears pears spears pears spears galloping lalloping
jalloping calloping kalloping jalloping lalloping galloping not too
sinister but a little. Bright and light,bright and light. Oh riding and
fighting,riding and fighting like a participial encounter of hetero-
plastic avariciousness. Tempered,I hope. Yes,tempered. Thank god.
Pardon me,thank God,I am so sorry. Well it was riding and closer
and it was a he and in shining armor quite dazzling and dizzling
and dizzying but not to him. Equilibrium. Gaiety. Only the gay is
equilibrious is gay and/or the equilibrious is gay is equilibrious?
But equally equilibrious? You are here be glad.

He rode and rode continuously,inexpressibly continuously,and
stopped for rest every now and then. Too often then and not
often now but just often enough. Yes,sometimes. Yes,sometimes
he fell off now and then when he had ridden too long but it was
not serious it was gay yes it was not serious because it was him if
it had not been him or if it had ceased to be him it would have
become serious and rather frightening but it was always him and
he always picked himself up and got back on his horse and rode on
a bit and then he got off when he chose to get off and then he
rested when he chose to rest; he never rested when he fell off be-
cause he said yes it is too degrading if I rest when I fall off,is much
too degrading and frightening,is not rest at all,is exhausting,I shall
rest now. WHENEVER I DAMN WELL PLEASE.

That was not the end of that,that continued into this so that is
not surely that any more than this is surely this because only he
knows and he does not say and I am glad for that because it is
too wearying for us,well for us all,to know and it is better to con-
jecture as I know that we understand in a way that is ours and
we would be unhappy to understand in a way that is any one
elses even if it were his and we were understanding him which is
not at all probable. It might become terribly mixed up.

It is inextricably weaving with the present in the present in a rather weben und schweben or webend und schwebend way that is comforting and comfortable and promising and fulfilled,like one great and seeing eye which is not always the case but is in this case oh very fortunately and we are all quite happy because we have just heard four saints sing in three acts but one of them is extra making three saints and there is one that is double making four again but there is no mistaking no mistaking that there are four acts and they are acts to be subdivided and there are scenes and arias and recitatives and it was all grand and we are happy still although it is over because it is never ended and that eye is still on it is on and it is seeing it is on you,and to you from you it is on him,but to you it is on you,and I would be happy and I certainly would be comfortable and comforting and fulfilled and promising and it is on you and we are pleased and then you can and may if you wish stop for a rest and for rest,you if you wish may rest now,get off and rest and we know,you may get off and rest and we know that the eye is still seeing and it will wait while you rest and then up and away,up and away,and we,we will,we all will,know that it is still you and that you have not not been you and that you have not ceased to be you and that you are still you and that you are rested and that you are on your way,and we,we will,we all will,be glad,and we will say that it is you and we know that it is still you and that we believe,yes we believe,it is quite tremendous and exciting and complimentary to all concerned,we believe that you will and shall remain you and only you.

[May 25, 1947]

52

LINES IN IMITATION OF AN ELDER POET
WHOSE NOSTRUM MAY BE SAID TO BE HIS MARE

(*to Robert Sherwood*)

The rugged twilight bumps between
my horse's shafts (a bit obscene)
and I, perforce, must journey now
to tell the horsey why, and how:
"Horsey, my horse, my horse," say I,
"the twilight trots in yonder sky
and kicks the bluejays as they fly,
and trods the sun and trods the moon
and trods the clematis in June.
It dashes from the morning room
as if the sun had held a broom
and yet would be surpassing hurt
to find itself compared with dirt!
If on this country road weren't we,
the twilight would unnoticed be:
electric lights are cowards, yet
a man's a man for all of thet."

My horse had nodded now and then
so I was not astounded when
he turned his head, and over his shoulder,
kicking aside a neighbor's boulder,
remarked in tones of moderation
the following modest observation:
"Ability to think and see
is found in you, me, and the flea."

POEM

Arrow, arrow
is so dark
and leaning broken
through the air
beats, leafy,
the sky.

Pinions, pinions
lie down in tin,
silver and green.

An apple in the yard
is your own heaven
mother, frequent not
the orchard.

Apples, apples
disguise how often,
its tendrils twitching,
the earth burns
at night.

A SUITE OF VOWELS

1. POPULAR SONG

Coo woo soo boo!
Hippy dippy hippy dee.
Lulu, lulu ach! mafooloo,
lala, pala, lala, whee!

Lara tiara, spiffy spiff
what wot what wot what wot, poo —
essa, essa, essa, lulu,
caramba, colomba, calliope!

Fa, fa, fa, fa
fah! ist ist, ist eek!
La la, lulu, lala Schmerz;
lulu luvlu, lulu bee!

2. VARIATION ON A STANZA OF SHELLEY

Iloo iloo allah ow i illuff
uh en ee ee, oo ee an oof
i oo; uh oh uff oh ee ess.
Oo i op up ow ach vow i,
oh e oh e oh an i op
ih ed oh an all ah oo oh.

3. VARIATION ON A SONNET OF WORDSWORTH

Um oh oo-i, ach iss oo-i,
at ih oo i oo i at ih
ov aw at ih ov aw trelaw.
So bene bissy bissy beh,
so bene bissy booh boo beh.
Ah ih at it ah ih
ah o at oh ah a ah at
oom ih um ih oh oh ho oh
oom ih at it ih at.
Um ah at um oom um
ih eh ah ih ih eh
so bene bene ih ih ih
ih at et at ihih ah
so bono bene ih ih sah.

4. POPULAR SONG

Trooloo bulu bulu booloo ga-bash!
Issitoo issitoo issgoomplash.
Tirra lirra tirra tart,
issy boo issy bah issy iss bash!

Lassiti lassiti lassiti poo
issull bih putt pash
issull bih putty poo.
Whah issitoo dash barash
pa ra ra ra rarara lash!
pa ra ra ra rururu pash!
iss iss bissy boo
tirra lirra tirra ga-bash!

THESEUS

I have not met you often
only at certain dangerous stiles
where the water lapped wool from between my toes
as I leaped full-bodied and aromatic
into the linen branches of apple trees
or clumped as if I might soon and easily die of gout.
And I've seen you at the movies
beneath the ripely tangled marquee
strolling sensationally arm-in-arm with a mannequin
toward the ticket-taker
who sifts motion with a stub.

Often you might have noticed
my body in any display window
draped in the tweed of a marvelous travel poster
whispering words of foreign poets
to a disinterested mother.
Indolent in silk you have stroked the nose of a horse
but eyes have followed
with threads tracing thoroughly
the many alleys, offices and lavatories of the city
and my committed flesh
seeks the free wilderness
unable to force you as you lie in innocent sloth.
My cries have dictated
your heroic discipline:
I sing to wake you in a death that I may flower.

A PROCESSION FOR PEACOCKS

The devil upon the flower
is black
as the stable of choked bracken
house of the ink-soaked horse
whose wings spread night to smother the quickest dancer.

At best I have begged
o whirling generation of foreign gods
only your uninterested gardens in the dark flesh!

Kneel with me
among the strawberries and pumpkin seeds of
our childhood
to vie with animals
in meaning evil.

I stroke the bush
that hides your hair, delay of silver birds on
twigs of strings
opal eyes that squint and twist
to the cold moon,
and flaccid limbs resign the city in blue rest and ruin.

What eyelash kisses
and what memoried plant
escapes
the dampness of the dream?
The strings are slack
mushrooms wading alone
toward the lips at the back of the sun, toward the hips.
O breasts of fungus.

                    I shall hold my self like a basket of vegetables
fresh-picked
                    in faultless adolescence
                    for the efficacy of legends
                    and gods
                    is in me
among the saffron-cheeked people who blush like thorns and weep
                    a purple bush.
                    Sticky the leaves of their eyes
                    and warm the tongues
                    that smooth my voice
and polish me to burning sun-stemming song!

                    At night they carry me
                    in a palanquin of twigs
                    as if I were a bruisable pear,
                    soft as the sunrise
                    their voices pry my way
                    through the dark.

In a cuisine of thighs they dance the rhythmic flesh of gods
                    made gods through joy
                    and prancing darkly
                    create.

                    White is white
                    from teat to knee
                    and your strong plumage against my cheek wields
its grace
                    like a red wind.

                    As the song between the teeth, scarcer than apples
and more brilliant
                    than a tree of Christian ornaments
                    sips,
o what a glowing basin for trumpets, harps and xylophones!
                    What pressure of the keys
                    ripe pear in a box of chalcedony!

I am stamped of your flesh
like a handbill or snake.
After the deluge
you fly to me, weary dove or hamstrung eagle
with covered eyes
and angel pinions.

Suckled by your breath
and clasped by your ravens
in a litter of sheets and sparks
o dam of the forests, oval torrent, heart of my blood, I
see these squares upon squares arise
and our jewels
like splitting angles
shriek in the white light of the secret sun!

[THY SNAKES ARE SWOLLEN]

Thy snakes are swollen
and my feet are sore.
Where are Thy waters, o Zion?

Thy fruits bear bruises
and my knees are scabbed.
Where are Thy waters, o Zion?

Thy sky's a coward
while my blue eyes drown.
Where are Thy waters, o Zion?

Thy saints are faggots
but flesh alone burns!
Where are Thy waters, o Zion?

GOD!

This isn't the first time I've wet my pants,
so stop bellowing and tell me the weather forecast.
I'm so tired of looking out this window, or is it
a cupola? What usually tires me is doors.

This room is about as small as a meadow
because the sun makes a pumpkin look like an apple,
but my real concern is with the clouds, you
wet your pants and I'll wet mine. The weather

is a great ruiner. And the way you've backed
these window panes with silver isn't very nice.
What have you done to the door? I'm so sick
of velvet! Get your elbow out of the clock.

If I ever have to look at you again I'm liable
to pull a purple quilt over my head, roll my eyes
until I fall flat on my back, and then, tired
and cross, sneeze myself to death. Pfui!

TO LOVER, TO GOD

To Lover

This
    wickedness
        which
            you
                have
                    made
                        me
                          do
                            my
                              mother
                                observed!

To God

My   mother   made   me

do   wickedness   which   you   have   observed

LISTEN, MY ENEMIES . . . .

Invariably, holding a ball,
I fear death from some direction.

A NOTE TO HUGH AMORY

Listen, you mad poet, never
ask for gasoline from the girl
selling bonbons in the department store!
she faints dead away as the sea
from your lips bursts over the glass
stuffed with nylons and nougatines
bushelled in chrome like eggs on ice
to invade the Belgians by ear.

Words, words, words! the floorwalker
yanks your buttonhole, kicks at your face
as the building falls inward to know
at last some part of what the stone
is. Your words, sea-rushed engines,
hammer on, and from the muck
and bones and golden curls and silk
your sienna house, New Jerusalem,
rises. Art! Hosanna! Huzzah!

FOR EDWARD GOREY

The picture is the miracle, not
just the fearless fact alive.
What anger you assume as weapon
in your fight for order
rends you but the effort
bears. Upon the void you scratch
your signature as special:
you people this heatless square
with your elegant indifferent
and your busy leisured
characters who yet refuse
despite surrounding flames
to be demons. You arrange
on paper life stiller than
oiled fruits or wired twigs
in canvas bowls, even though
the resemblance is human.

See how upon the virgin grain
a crosshatch claws a patch
of black blood unsuspected
in that sterile barnyard.
You transfigure hens, your men
cluck tremulous, detached;
at sunrise they avert their beaks.
And when the sun goes down
their eyes glow gas jets
and the gramophone supplies them,
resting, soft-tuned squawks.

MORGENMUSIK

for Jerome Rubenstein

1 What lancers pierce the air,
   what shrieks assemble the morning?
   I'm couched on laurel
   poisoned by Apollo's hate,
   the vase beneath my head's abrim
   with cobras and cupidity,
   and this my morgenmusik's played
   by healthy raping soldiers
   on the prettily reacting skins
   of giddy boys, prenatal idiots
   whose mothers were affrighted by
   a tiff among the gods
   and found no sacrament nor lemon-juice
   would bleach the fear
   from nipples glowing green.

2 Awake and weep, I say awake
   and weep; the sob's the thing
   that made Greek tragedy;
   the sob is general, native to
   the human and inhuman heart,
   life's only sure attainment.
   Pan was silly but Apollo knew
   how many times to strike his lyre
   to tease a tear, and many times
   he struck an inundation
   from teutonic matrons
   with discernment in their veins
   and a worry for a heart.
   They listened in the morning
   and they knew. Attend.

3 Beat the drum slowly, break
the ivory ribs; these are no
elephants and this no burial,
this acre underneath my window's
far from secret; and who
has ever bothered leaving
the body of a boy intact?
We must get used to beating bones
to forks and spoons again,
forget they're human bones,
practice a falsetto lilt
that's only partly keen,
appreciate a different kind
of drum and fifes made out of shins,
confess things to each other,
dance the Männerdämmerung un-
prejudiced, with discipline and taste.

A SENTENCE

At Kent or Sweetwater
where the tumbleweeds
and boxwoods sing
in cartwheels and rows,
a miracle may occur
to Janus when he faints
in the tired sun's waves.

SEA CHANGES

1

As the ship pulls out
of the rind-strewn harbor
stevedores dock-loll
tired after labor;

a go-away basket
gunned with champagne
summons the salt wind's
gull, white champion!

and grey hills fall
apart like thighs.

2

There, as we breast the first breaker
that bursts from the crosscurrents of porpoise
and splays like an exploding tern
upon the shell of our immaculate ship,

we gather our strength like a whiplash or purpose
and push forward, brazen, into the barren
field of parachutes, butterflies and beakers,
as if the waves washed and fed our healthy shape.

3

Cormorants call after, where-away?
and canoes on lagoons mirror our goodby.
We swim in the gusting wind that steers to our cry
and hears the gold-bit day
roar in its ear as our voice!
Like a ship or chalice

full of yams and gums and chocolate and mercurochrome
our sails fill the hungry sky;
our ears hear high-
er than albatross songs of serpents, witches, deserts, death and home.

[IT SNOWS BEHIND MY EYES]

It snows behind my eyes
and it snows into the sea.

The orange trees are bitten
by a falling blight

Smudgepots smoke my lids
and bruise my sockets blue.

The sky is close as a bandage.
The strong sea licks my ear.

The oranges fall on the land
and float away, garbage.

NEW YORK

for George Montgomery

Fire so quick, that smash of pain
the stroke that fires the mountain
smashes puddles that burst like agony

or that weapon of mahogany
used by women who love too much
backwards themselves.

                    Men of such
persuasion need no instrument
to feed the flame.

              Mountains meant
once gods and now mean penises
while puddles once meant venuses,

now will not bear: bellies
round with scented jellies
which protect no child. In this dense city
Herrick's love's a deafened ditty.

AT THE THEATRE

O mon Bien! O mon Beau! Pirandello!
My tears moved the stage's whirlpool
up and down like a medicine ball.

I'd read the program, knew who
was really acting and who was not,
but his eyes and fingers flung their
judgments. My heart pulled out of

shape. I rose towards the stage on
sight lines like a perspective of
knowledge: "Dearest of kings, who am I?"
His hands fled to his hair. "Boy" he said

"you mistake the red spots on my cheeks
for images of eyes. Stare deeply, my back
is to a wilderness of air. Weep not.
Define, rather, the tigers that choose

and eat your heart. Or admire flowers
that gouge out their eyes to shame the rain."
I lay there sobbing under the lantern of
his one faithful servant. People in niches

sneered at my intrusion. The curtain
never fell. Mon Bien! mon Beau! "You've
made my life your flights and riches. But
dearest of kings! let me out of your mind!"

[Cambridge, May 1949]

71

FIRST NIGHT

to Lyon Phelps

All day the sun sang
we washed and swept and
did things to glasses

       the ivy crepitated like
       a faculty chamber but
       was our talkative room

We had the gin and the
onions and the hurry and
raced through the shower

       the guests were wild and
       happy knowing whose day
       it was ours of course

Our poet was late but
he was our poet we
shouted with glee already!

       he arrived looking
       worried were we worried
       yes we were children

The curtain rose like a
wing on a mountain as
noisily as all our heads

       this was our play the
       dancers had hold of the
       actors what would they do?

Our friend's heart lay
bare on the boards for us
and our anxious thanks

      to think of that act of
      love! that the Muse lit
      with our answer and joy

Shall we think of that
gift without a tear and
smile on hard prose days?

      the deed that made us
      worthy of its serious
      love toward everyone

                   [Cambridge, May 1949]

EPITAPHS

1 She died on a ranch near Tucson;
   she was going to have a baby and she died
   because her best friend told her
   no one loved her as much as she loved everyone.

2 You're worms' love now, you're whiter
   than you ever were before;
   I loved you as a virgin but
   I cannot say I love you any more.

3 Lie there, lie there
   breathe no sigh;
   lie there, lie there
   cars pass by;
   lie there, lie there
   there's no eye
   to make you feel uneasy.

4 Waiting under the grass
   for the presence of time to end,
   waiting under the grass
   for the passionate past to begin,

   waiting under the grass
   the body is cold,
   waiting under the grass
   a soul grows from mold.

5 Address the preacher's stentorian pride:
   I listened, but now I'm sorry I died.

6 My heart at the end of the pen
   is all that I can bear
   to talk about; my love
   my love I cannot bear
   to speak of you.

7 Elegant one, your frozen form
   is perfect now; your velvet lids
   and ice-grey compost skin are stronger
   than can be living iron will,
   timidity's bled out of you, your blushes
   drip from a chill mortician's altar.

8 Although the hour of death is past
   his hair is growing still, alas.

9 Here lies my daughter
and I grieve for her sins.

10 Many have changed from pulp to sand,
but summer remembers only her hand.

11 The age of anxiety is the best:
now laid in earth means laid to rest.

12   Here lies
Salathiel Pavy, beset in stealth
by enemies envious of his wealth;
heavenward now his soul's astride,
may god his stammer and squint abide.

13 The fresh cut-flowers begin to wilt,
the keening women cease their lilt,
moisture's sinking from open loam;
alone, alone I must go home.

14 O how the rain drops down
and bruises her too tender flesh!

15 I have walked too long to ever wish
that we might meet again.

[Grafton, June-August 1949]

PASTORALS

1

Goldenrod shot rusting through the fields ahead, and far to the
north horse-chestnut candles fucked the sun.

We followed the stream caressing salamanders and finally, lying
on a hillock, looked at fame our own blue sky.

We drowsed in sweaters, setting sun, needing the healthy bubbles
of a spa, summoning the sea; but frogs began to ache and fishes fell
upon the river bank, beat each other daintily in crowds, choked and
strangled.

We picked our way homeward through fish-blood, through bodies
on the newsprint beach.

2

Walking by water, at the harp's disgrace
we shuddered; the young girl
in her yielding bud echoed faintly
across our hearts' dawn-bandaged tremors.

A giggle, I pray you, a giggle for that girl's
painful scream in her first moment of love.

3

Pastures of error where the daintiness of our blood has felt
distress, pastures our impotence has clawed in shame only to have its
white flesh disgraced by the sobs of a grass lined with sable, pastures,
moving always over the hill, let us stray on your green belly once
more, let us once more play in the sun among your pubic flowers,
as our selves just come out of the trees!

4

Seizing the pattern of dismay we wrenched our knuckles glassy, bruised our knees together as our eyeballs touched. We kissed, our lips blue and dry as reindeer moss, stirring, springy, timid tongues of dead rabbits.

Swept through the orchard on the summer sand the ants were blemishes and bees were doves. This is real! I've put iodine on your finger! You'll never die now!

Yes I will; you may not, but I will.

So that as the time of harvest approached my heart felt heavy, a guilty lodestone. I began to hear dark murmurs in my ears and asked if the wind was not in the firs early this year.

No! The clouds never fall and we shall always laugh! run! sing!

But I required more bedclothes at night, and a warm porridge for breakfast; I practiced the piano a good deal; when I walked the fields my feet hurt.

Kiss me once again, love, before you die!

5

I have told you time after time that as we stare off into the blue mountains I can think only of spain, our blood-grimed and vulgar mistress.

I was twelve.

The trolley cars rolled across my eyeballs; larkspurs see you, lovers!

Consent to dance, with me, a fandango.

My knee is bloody, I've soiled your gown: it is because I was thinking of orange groves; there were two pieces of wood attached and as I knelt to pray the pulp and juice oozed out smelling of weddings and a heavenly choir of castrati lisped into my ear — their tongues so soft and smooth I could hear nothing!

O hear the songs of the matadors! What good are the books? I shall never pray again!

The bull charges across the sand, breasts dripping milk and balls clanging, but a needle in the eye means blindness. O my people! a lover's flower is pitiful on a tomb. The bull, black as a miner, falls, kneeling, to the yellow sands, recites his nada litany, and, cursing his conqueror, dies.

The tears of the Ebro are muddy this night!

See in the distance Pasionaria bathes the fields! The wounded stagger to each other and with a final stirring of the loins beget a human image lying over the hill to nurse our hopes.

6

Heat flares in the August breeze
and herons, late-wed, knock
their knees together
in the wind-piled water,
carolling like a dizzy clock;
heifers bushel lewdly in the trees,

so anciently that harmony is cool
to wade in, cool to sip. Wake
me, O god, your wet
herbaceous plumes fit
my wound close as cotton, make
soft disease of lust beside this eager pool.

I once burned houses better than
the Scandinavians, and at the touch
of flesh would quiver
like an adder: lover
I have crossed my heart with such
as parsley, burning cigarettes, and am again a man!

7

Who am I? And at what door, characteristic and unoblique, have I cached my soul under deciduous leaves?

It's all the same—a bush in the storm, a lost soul, Eliza crossing the ice, Alvan shot dead, laughter. "Don't you suppose some day everyone will be like us?" Bah! said the fly to the mosquito. I've no anguish left! I kissed my way through the Crimean War, you remember, and they all fell in love with Florence Nightingale.

No key fits: where love and honour gleam through the window, protected souls, I am a stranger. The beauty within me withers at my glance. I stand upright, whiphandle to jaw, betrayer of my race and mudguard of the bourgeoisie.

Listen to me, you who are attracted: the other dusk in the streets I was the gentlest person you know—my periwinkle irises dripped like the corners of a jackal's mouth. Love me!

Bring me my doll.

[Grafton, June-August 1949]

AT THE SOURCE

Morning's at the Hebe!
what a dish of grace
and partridges—whee!

I am very happy here.
My feet are washed clean,
Africans beat drums
and the gin is sweet.

Wherever else are such songs
bright in the jungle
and the water so clear?

Be bright, be bright!

[Cambridge, September 1949]

THE MAN WITHOUT A COUNTRY

Into every world walks the perfect being
once. Roman candles are his hautboys

and big things like pigeons and horses
float to his feet, pretending they are motes

in the sun. He's no Saint Francis though,
and his trip could not be called anabasis

just because he occasionally wears a beard.
There is that about him which does not meet

the eye, but he is obviously as pure and fierce
as electricity. Even Ignorance loves

his motives. What a cry there is when he passes
through the streets! Emerald dust whirls

in the air and holy water makes deltas
of cheeks—some think he's Jesus or Siegfried!

He's not. He turns his back in the sun to pose
for memory green thumb up. The moment's gone.

Some of the crowd are turned to salt. The rest,
like anxious Daniel, are enslaved by lions.

[Cambridge, October 1949]

PRINCESS ELIZABETH OF BOHEMIA, AS PERDITA

The delicate girl was eager to air
her virgin flower-de-luce held tight held
high in her fist as a poodle's nose, rare
as a garnished mushroom on a jewelled
Stuart's table. The startling innocence
of her eyes made the sky a rumpled bed,
her white skin was refined as th' excremence
of that delicious bird: the dove. Like Ed
walks o'er fresh fields in Scottish tweed, her stroll
widened the sense of heather. Negligence,
too, was her tour de force. A barcarolle
restored to each heart her adolescence:
    caught in her eyes the late years wept, seeing
    th' impossibility of her being.

[Cambridge, December 1949]

A RENAISSANCE PORTRAIT OF THE AUTHOR

A courtier strides along, his feathers
straightening in the breeze. His boon
has been denied. From his clenched left
fist extends a mountain range as grim
as Atlas. He mutters so coherently that
a quartet of wind instruments is darkly
visible at the edge of the forest. He
puffs his cheeks to snort angrily but
the clouds scurry away in tatters.

Upon the right the brightness of the
court defies my technique, tingling
with business at the defeated courtier's
shoulder. The queen is leaning out
a casement kissing pigeons while
a smiling lady holds the queen's clean
coif. The green pride at his feet glares,
forbids the courtier's looking back.
On his nape he bears the azure whole.

And the frivolous hunting party romp
at his mercy! He could easily topple
their trees with a kick of his velvet
right foot. A hand on his rapier betrays
a motive his hooded eyes and beardless
face will not easily resolve. Thoughts
eager as the hawk that pins the castle
to the sky flourish on pure spleen. Ah!
the sea behind his codpiece brews poison.

VARIATIONS ON A THEME BY SHELLEY

1
We live in an opal or
crystal ball. The sun's
an eye, against it clouds
crowd like Spanish castles
on a mountain. Everywhere
colors dampen cling and from
our heat slide into the sky.

2
The shifting roses
of brick and iron
bleed the earth as
we erect trellises
ladders and trees.

3
I don't want my poems
lisped on the numbered
tongues of children. May
they be part of the world
and sight by which we
become the eye and defy
questions with our beauty.

TRAVEL

Sometimes I know I love you better
than all the others I kiss it's funny

but it's true and I wouldn't roll
from one to the next so fast if you

hadn't knocked them all down like
ninepins when you roared by my bed

I keep trying to race ahead and catch
you at the newest station or whistle

stop but you are flighty about
schedules and always soar away just

as leaning from my taxicab my breath
reaches for the back of your neck

[Boston, April 1950]

[IN PERIL OF MY LIFE AT THE HANDS]

In peril of my life at the hands
of these cuspidors & pinball machines
oh my dearest love! I call out to you
to hold tight the wire though it cut
your fingers.
    When I get back I'll
tell you about my far arrival,
whether I was sweaty or not and how
much weight I lost on the trip; if my jackknife
had blood on it and my feet hurt;
and how it looked: like a turtle to be hauled
into the boat or a parasol to be bravoed,
or your bed that I had to break so
it would be safe & natural for us to lie

I'll keep my balance and beat the pulse[?]
If your love & hand hold steady
Around the lover from the Continental
So thoughts grow like feathers, the dead end of life?

Were I an older poet I would have already written
a portrait of a lady about you.
You are serious. Like a Victorian lampshade.
What discipline would suit you? Alexandrines, I suppose.
Something rigid, with sudden quirks hidden,
Something rather rough, form that turns out to be glasses[?]

AMERICA

Is it Cato Seneca or Cicero
who stands with his back
(across the grass) towards
Columbus? through the trees
and the green light comes
Ulysses smiling and stretching forth
his black hand (a saucy
Samaritan) to save Redskins
and Whitefolk from de-
portation   Gravely walking
he takes us from the Roman
(forget Catiline who-
ever you are) and leads us
to Columbus   A 7-Up
truck roars by (bellow-
ing Swanee) so we hoist
Ulysses on our shoulders
and shout Hooray!   Columbus!

[Boston, June/July 1950]

ANOTHER AMERICAN POEM

I wakened! at the first tap
of morning, its light fingernail
ticked off my eyeball and
with a clap of felt erasers
like a sob in grammar school
I saw my flesh as chalk. All
this, while the birds hurried
into each other's mouths amidst
the leaves, and babies strangled
in Doctor Dentons. Quickly,
insistently, hoping against
hope, I waited for the light
to change, but there was no
place to advance to, the North
was blinding, I was too white
for the South, Redskins
hadn't really been driven
from the West. Oh Columbus,
what you started! the trains
are always on time, the
honeysuckles are sentimental
and only the college athletes
really do something. If
conversion symptoms and
the daily press are right
it's a great comfort to
think of flesh as grass.
Let us fall to our knees and,
in the words of Al Capone
perhaps? go straight to hell.

A LITANY

Night sweet are you
as a cloud lying
between our eyes
kissing our forehead
with reverence and
I mean anyone's.

You night entertain
us like an acrobat
strutting in pink
absentmindedly in love.
The stars—yellow and
glass—figure out

problems in arithmetic
while we know not what
elephants think. They
look on dispassionately
as if we were at a
circus. It's our show.

The warmth of night
ignores our gesture—
like the boy from Moon
who sings as a woman
in love with cups of
sake—or almost nothing.

The circus sinks quickly
because we look too
hot and there's no work
tomorrow. No bearings
to be taken and the
home is every back.

Before morning we may
be equal to our forehead
bending back by logarithm
to touch dutifully the
abyss. Because it's black.
To pay a debt. To rest.

So elephants disappear
on the softest shoulders.
Inquire into our motives
o night! and put up signs.
Strut no vengeance! think
up a breeze from, say,

Siam. In your attack on
Aldebaran use our straight
shooting and be pleased
with our planet unknown
elephants and all. Oh
don't be lazy or funny

night! and dictate no
eye in the middle of our
forehead. Our brothers
did not invent fire.
We love you as you are.
Our quarry. Our corollary.

[Boston, July 1950]

MEDITATIONS ON MAX ERNST'S *HISTOIRE NATURELLE*

Seven Prose Poems

INTRODUCTION

It is true that ferocious lions, all lions, scent succulence, and one may add scent succulence lasciviously, delicious word. It is also true that at the same time lime trees grow tractably, especially on the boarded plains, and most especially when within hearing of the sniffing lions. But no matter what happens we, as vegetable spirits, fall to our knees before the beauty of nature (how we sniff and enlarge our sensibility!) because of nature and our knowledge of nature.

This is why we love washing machines (those mirrors of apple blossoms) and looms (the progenitors of nudes) and airplanes (memorials to our fathers). In the same way the films have taught us how beautiful we really are from the anguish of our shadows and the accuracy of objects (the heart of Charlie Chaplin). All machines, similarly, enliven us. We face the world with self-respect as well as love. We are no longer hypocritically humble, nor ignorantly proud.

To certain men we owe this liberation of our spirits. Nature herself is grateful, divulging her inmost secrets with frightening prodigality, so that words fill their mouths, the brushes push every-which-way in their hands, and the notes cram their ears. Genius is eagerness as well as everything else.

And sometimes our meditations may enlarge their truth. It is possible. Like a stroke of luck. A discovery. More art.

THE SEA AND THE RAIN

Gone. Yes, quite gone. No, I have not looked, nor do I care to go to any window, no matter whose, nor do I
    care. This is how it is done. Place your hand close to your eye; now the other hand on top. You, dearest of all, hold the sledge-

hammer over
near the door. Like a tom-tom, pretend. Your legs must flutter
and with incredible speed we pass through Orion. My
darling! Orion is strangling your heart!
Do not leave me.

A GLANCE

September came quietly. The trees wound around me so decorously.
It was like an initiation.
"Are you a cannibal?"
"My mother . . ."
"Answer me!"
The leaves settled about the trees in an even more profound
circle. How was I to know? There were hints of war and every-
where I looked girls were taking jobs in factories. I had done
nothing. I pride myself on my innocence. Even that is completely
gratuitous. Like the rain.
Please. No more longing, yearning, words fail me, my poor
fool,
care for yourself, you are dying.
It is up to god to pray for the dead. That is what privilege
means
is it not?

LITTLE TABLES AROUND THE EARTH

I am very much afraid of a fissure. A cold wind blows down the
back of my neck, yes, just where leprosy first attacked me
and now my flock lies all about me, woolly with the stuff. Do
not disturb me. I shall press my forehead firmly to the earth
for I shall soon be blind. Hum something, will you?
Nearest of all, my father told me, warned me, of the conse-
quences
how passion wells up like a tornado of spiraling blood so that

the tongue barely can move its thickness into the mouth of another
   and the ear grows hair to hide its shape. Have you ever thought
of how far away we are from each other? all your hair between us,
all your flesh
   and the whole air.

ICEFLOWER SHAWL AND GULF STREAM

Be as rich as you wish and as grand as you want and do grow as
fast as you can! They are after you, make no mistake about that
   because there are so many ruses, so many minds.
   Do you remember the story of the fauns, how they ran until
they fell 'neath the arrows of a Khan? Jenghiz or perhaps one even
more terrible? Do not pray
   you will bleed anyway, it is terrible to see the stars in the sky
   and to feel the earth underneath you rock with laughter!

EARTHQUAKE

I am horrified that you affront and confound me! Are you
insane?
   I deny in order to affirm. Slough off the old skin in order to
sun my flesh. I wander alone about the earth among these people
whom I love and would not burden them
   no! would not!
   and would not build a god; I shall find myself, find the form
my experience demands
   clamors for! It is that I seek:
   self. You see, you know.
   Experience. Is it not
   self?

THE PAMPAS

Yes, follow me, love me

   like a faithful bird. I am as capable of smiling as the next and
you will find my cough echoing in your mind through the years
of our annihilation and distemper.

   Being lovers, our problem is space not time. I want your eyes
to be just behind my ears, your buttocks slightly beneath my navel,
without room to sigh.

   Distance! you are the vision, the elegance, oh! the grandeur of
our disease. As flesh rots away from flesh, diminishing, vanishing,

   you make it seem the fault of the years.

HE WILL FALL FAR FROM HERE

Let us say that the poet, wherever he is in our thoughts, has taken
things into his own hands. You see the danger. Either a colossus
or a louse. Can we bear not to understand? We are not stones. Un-
fortunately, petulantly.

   In his imagination do we gather no moss? Or do we promenade
incessantly and inescapably the vistas of the Carcere?

   He opened the pages for me, they fell before my eyes like great
squares of flesh, empty as piazzas. There were, however, no pali-
sades. The wind seemed to warn, "Honi soit . . ."

   who?

   but I felt no breeze, and my skin is extremely sensitive. We are
dealing with literature, I reminded myself. Fear puts one off.

   The poet felt that it was too high or too far away, obviously,
from the way he was breathing. A bitter prince. On one side the
light disappeared, was completely swallowed up;

   on the other it glared blue. It frightened me even though I was
not in the picture. Perhaps, kept running through my mind. Alter-
native is too young a word for a poet. I became afraid that he
would confess something about his sister, to me. And the page
was still blank before my eyes. His lips began to move but all I
could hear was a wind. He obviously felt articulate. Reader, I must
hasten to you,

   save me!

OTHER WRITING

A JOURNAL: October-November 1948 & January 1949

10/8/48

I wonder if the course of narcissism through the ages would have been any different had Narcissus first peered into a cesspool. He probably did. At any rate a cesspool is a pool, and there is a unity to narcissism which hopelessly binds through time and space. Every time I inhale a cigarette I look hastily toward the floor: and some day I shall see, to my horror, a serpentine head drag the jeweled back-shell of a tortoise toward the radiator.

Read Camus' two plays, *Caligula* and *Cross Purpose*; the latter rather obvious, the former magical. Also finished *The Rector* today, Mrs Oliphant is charming.

It seems that talent and genius are ever opposed to taste. How can one rant at Cocteau's less pertinent bits of ingeniousness when he does something like *The Eternal Return*? As he says in the preface to *The Typewriter*, or infers, it is, apart from whether one is writing obvious plays subtly, or subtle plays obviously, a matter of expedience as well as compulsion to create a work of art; the artist attempts to give his time what it needs, and his judgment is the factor which dictates his success; the artist is aware that nothing is begun or ended definitely; caught in the flood of destruction which is our historical milieu, he wonders where to place his sandbag most efficaciously; if his judgment is wrong, at least he stood on the levee, at least he used his judgment, at least he had a sandbag. No matter how much practice in judgment the artist gets, the slightest variation in situation throws him off from producing real art; the man of taste appreciates and even (yes!) condones the work of the past; he strolls historical levees and knows just where and why the floods were held in check; but he does NOTHING for his times! No matter what Cyril Connolly says it does not seem that Cocteau really *needed* opium to make him serious.

Much as I loved *The Shaving of Shagpat*, I cannot understand why André Gide should be *jealous* of Meredith over it; Gide could never in the world have written (nor could anyone else have) it, but not only that, Gide shouldn't even desire to have written it.

10/9/48

Roast tongue reminds me of kissing, yes.

Poetry is an impulse toward Armageddon. Prose is the kiss of the enemy.

One keeps a journal so that one writes, as one must, all the time.

I am reading, slowly, Saint Jerome, and I know now that Satan lives, and I have not yet made up my mind which side I am on.

Henry Miller is our 20th century Wordsworth.

10/11/48

Utter depression. Listened to Schumann (piano concerto, piano quintet, 2nd symphony) over and over. Dame Myra Hess is so successful with Schumann because of her sweet nobility, peculiar to the British, and often their most annoying national trait.

I ran away to Boston and bought the Scott-Moncrieff translation of *The Red and the Black* yesterday. The bookstore's proprietress is a wizened sixty-odd in a red wig; small physique and tiny movements like a bantam hen. The bookstore smells of food (she eats her lunch there). The books are all dusty and teeter in their precarious piles when one is touched. Thousands of books that someone was contented to read only once, a few that someone hated to sell. A friend of the proprietress came into the store looking for back issues of antique magazines; a woman of fifty, well-dressed but shabby, who may or may not have washed her face that morning. She talked of not having been able to subscribe to antique magazines since her husband's death, of having to sell her collection of antique magazines because there wasn't room in her new quarters for them. Now she wanted to look up some old antique pieces in order to get an idea of their worth. I didn't raise my head or move but when she became aware of me reading she announced that she had no books to sell; she was giving all her books away so that she could be sure the people she wanted to have them *would* have them; she said "giving" with a splendid pride. As she was leaving the two women discussed in low voices where the best food was to be had most reasonably, and the visitor recommended the roast beef at a nearby cafeteria. It had begun to rain when I left, but all Huntington Avenue smelled of disintegrating books. As far as I could see the sidewalks teemed with nightbound people, looking for something or anything. They didn't seem to care too much what they found, so elaborately had they prepared themselves for disappointment, and the rain, lit by store windows, glittered down on them. I didn't write this last night because it didn't seem worth the bother to write at all.

10/12/48

Have just returned from Yom Kippur services, the first time I had ever attended.

"All vows and self-prohibitions, vows of abstinence and promise, vows with self-imposed penalties and payments, which we may vow, swear, promise, and devote, from this day of Atonement unto the next day of Atonement (may it come to us in happiness), we repent them all; may they be held by the Almighty of no moment. May such vows be by Him not considered as vows, nor such oaths as oaths, nor such promises as well as obligations as binding. May they be all null and void, without power or binding force."

To think that the *Kol Nidre* had to be revived as spiritual protection against coercion by Christian savages! To think that it has remained in constant use these two thousand years! Our guilt stays in our blood, passed down generation to generation, like syphilis.

10/13/48

The world is inside my head, spinning slowly.

10/14/48

Sir Francis Bacon's message: manners maketh queens, but you have to change your underwear to really get anywhere.

Writers who share something: Mrs Oliphant, Howard Overington Sturgis, Mrs Inchbald, E M Forster, Maria Edgeworth.

A word of advice to the needy: lotuses are cheaper in the long run, and last for ages, just ages.

I wonder what the garbage man will give the world December 25th.

10/17/48

Waiting for the train I hear the whistle and run away. (It's true, you know—even with taxis!)

I often wish I had the strength to commit suicide, but on the other hand, if I had, I probably wouldn't feel the need. God! Can't you let us win once in a while?

The ordinary, the functional, the indispensable, man, the man who makes the world go round, is the only thing in life worth bothering about. What we need are bigger and better comfort stations. Shakespeare wrote with a remarkable lack of taste. Both Byron and Shelley wrote to be patronized by their inferiors. I loathe Henry Miller most, next to myself, and Marcel Proust most next to us. Cyril Connolly is silly; I wish both Caligula *and* Mr Sartre (being so alike) had died during adolescence (a fate which the latter may yet fulfill). If George Eliot had had any real talent she would have anticipated *The Well of Loneliness*. But I don't mean a word of it because MR GEORGE MEREDITH IS GOD! And it was nice of him to let me know.

10/18/48

If one could manage not to think. Life might become bearable. The less one thought, the less one might mind anything. If one never thought one would never care to write; one would never have anything to write.

10/19/48

Holidays coming. What will happen this year? Will I die capriciously? Or will it be something unexpected? Who killed the ivy on the mantle while we were away last Christmas vacation? Is there a god? Or was it the biddy?

We have no ivy to kill this year, haha.

10/24/48

The impulse, the, at times, compulsion, toward normalcy must be avoided, when its fulfillment is known to be unsatisfactory, and when the level of endeavor is, as it is by definition, inferior to that possible through idiosyncratic behavior. One must live in a way; we must channel, there is not time nor space, one must hurry, one must avoid the impediments, snares, detours; one must not be stifled in a closed social *or* artistic railway station waiting for the train; I've a long long way to go, and I'm late already. What is known as the normal social day-to-day existence is successful in only two ways: it passes the time, it stifles the creative impulse.

I find my thoughts returning constantly to the poor woman at the head of a chapter of *Melmoth the Wanderer* who

" . . . . . . sat, and thought
of what a sailor suffers."

Presumably she is leading a sad, sedentary life in a poem by, if I remember, Cowper.

10/25/48

Rain today; good and cold and raw; walked by the river after finishing *In Our Time*: wet feet, wet hair, cold eyes, excitement.

Hemingway's problem is not mine, whether he solved it successfully or not I can learn little from him. It is so far removed from me that I scarcely know what it is or how successful he is: the problem would seem to be (with the help of Malcolm Cowley) that of reducing (and I consider it a reduction) reality to simple enough terms for him to deal with in a literary (but before that privately in an emotional and intellectual) way; this is, I suppose, where the ritual comes in, ritual being the simplification in concrete terms of a complex belief or situation; in literature, as in religion, it seems to me that ritual ends up as elegant machinery. I disapprove of elegant machinery, and I disapprove more of the machinery than the elegance, possibly because of a desire to control my own predilections for both. Anyhow I'm tired of the current fad for short stories which clack along like a sewing machine dispensing pertinent information in stitches and stopping only when the garment is finished. I'd rather read someone's last will and testament. I want to move toward a complexity which makes life within the work and which does not (necessarily, although it may) resemble life as most people seem to think it is lived. If I am successful this should not need to be received as exotic or phantastic. The only simplicity I want is that of a coherent thing, a result of the work-as-a-whole's integrity. I must commence tonight to kiss *Nightwood* before going to sleep. If I must abandon characters to do this, then I must; it might be amusing to do it anyway. But it won't be necessary if I can avoid creating character as such, and only develop character in terms of the story, like puppets manipulated for effect. This makes my models *Between the Acts, Nightwood, The Tragic Comedians* (in a special way), *The Waves* (most of all, perhaps), *Ulysses,* and *Prothalamium;* also in a special way Ronald Firbank's perfect light tragedies *The Flower Beneath the Foot, Sorrow in Sunlight* and the less perfect because less light *Eccentricities of Cardinal Pirelli.* But in *Ulysses* and in *Prothalamium,* and in that other work I reverence, *Light in August,* we have ritual of a high and special sort; BUT: ritual as a result (of design, rhetoric, symbolism, pace, significance) rather than as a means to achieve another very different end. Ritual is bestowed on a work of art by its audience-participants as a response to the work's power and content, it is not put in, or made use of, by the author. For the reader to be involved in ritual is for him to say, "This work is an experience of something which I would rather receive through this artistic medium than through the direct apprehension of the thing itself." The writer does not create this response deliberately, at least not often, but rather it is a measure of his success in the work itself. So often the direct way of doing a thing is ruinous; try to grab the trout and it always gets away. The artist must make his work as perfect as possible, and trust that out of the welter of intentions, some will come clear and mean something to someone. And that is a high enough hope for anyone.

This confusion! My own writing is so far in the future that it may well be a mirage. Except that the future itself is a mirage and I refuse to disbelieve in either.

What would one give (one's soul?) to have written just a single meditation from the *Devotions Upon Emergent Occasions*! And the sermons, more beautiful than any of his poems . . .

10/26/48

I must take pains not to *intend* anything but the work itself, to let the work take shape as it comes (as the best of Anais Nin does, despite her self-imposed difficulties) and develop into an entity without interruptions or stumble-posts; I must think only of and for the emergent work and not allow messages or ideas as such to displace the validity of the work with their sham importance and subtle derangement of emphasis. The social novel is a scrapbook, the thesis novel a pamphlet.

The other enemy: style.

Works which deal with developing character, with exploring mental states, with preaching, can never be more than what they set out to do. (Dickens comes to mind as refutation: but his novels are novels first, afterward they have characters which live *within* the novel ((it is this that gives them their immortality—the character which can be abstracted from his setting is perishable)), and even further afterward we notice such things as social commentary, etc.; if Dickens wrote to develop character he is guilty of undisciplined caprice, if he wrote to reform society he seems to me, despite his influence on contemporary social attitudes, to have been the victim of a wayward and simple mind.) The artist works and his preoccupations appear in the work inadvertently; only the inferior artist, or the non-artist, needs the artificial stimulus of intent. We must return to the primitivism of making magic to go forward; whether he wants to or not the artist usurps the prerogative of the Primary Mover; he is his own First Cause. The artist thumbs his nose at gods, unless he, like Tolstoy, loses his nerve.

And again: there is no subject of true literature.

10/27/48
He is so deliberately not good, he probably will end up a saint.

In a journal are the things which would intrude on the purity of the work.

10/28/48
Inscription for a Christmas card: the vicious and the addled kneel to Jesus Christ tonight.

Maurice had devoured twelve custards before he realized that his was that peculiar kind of appetite which seeks first to curdle what it hopes later to digest.

10/29/48
Oh I hate myself and I'm afraid to die!

Horace McCoy's Gloria had at least the courage of her lack of conviction.

I sat in the Waldorf this morning between 16th Century and Chaucer classes and drank coffee and read *The Daily Worker* and thought of failure. I want so to write something good that I hate everything that is good unless it forces me to admire it (like *The Answer to Question Thirty Three* has just done). I am delighted every time a new book comes out that is a lemon, and if it is less than wonderful I try to obliterate its good points to myself by inner (and often audible) vituperation.

On the other hand I have, for my own projected works and ideas, only the silliest and dewiest of hopes; no matter what, I am romantic enough or sentimental enough to wish to contribute something to life's fabric, to the world's beauty, and how easy must Bergotte have rested with his books to commemorate him; simply to live does not justify existence, for life is a mere gesture on the surface of the earth, and death a return to that from which we had never been wholly separated; but oh to leave a trace, no matter how faint, of that brief gesture! For someone, some day, may find it beautiful!

To Rilke: Has the dove, then, no nostalgia, and the gull no bitterness?

To Gide: Prayer is not a discipline; prayer is a debauch.

11/2/48

Beginning for a movie scenario: The screen is blank; there is music (by Ernst Toch). The screen fills with fuchsia satin: the camera is nosing the flowery folds of a large bustle precariously riding the agitated rump of an angry young lady. We hear her saying, "I never will, and I'm glad to find myself, at this point, completely incapable of such a thing. He is despicable and degrading; I owe nothing to the Purble family name. In a word: NO!" There is a heave of bustle and the screen blackens like a bruised eye.

We are looking up a street: noon light, early spring. A row of street lamps like sick tulips blooms metallically in the sun as a speck on the distant stretch of sidewalk grows larger, approaches. It is a man in his early thirties wearing a restrained simper, a lavender tie, and such an elegant stroll that he might almost have gone to school with Harold Acton. He is humming a song of his own composition entitled *Your Room Is Awfully Pleasant But I Think I'll Run Along*; it is, of course, Gerard Purble, and as his eyes roll about with what we immediately recognize is an habitually avid curiosity the camera takes over their action, scooting under taxicabs, into store windows, peering into faces, down bodices, hurrying here, lingering there, distorting features and accidentals (to be worked out in detail), etc.; Gerard Purble is chatting with himself in jovial tones: "There is a certain satisfaction in being so good, so dimly and conventionally good, that it gives acute pain to everyone who comes in contact with you. I am the sort of person Savonarola would have adored intemperately . . . . ."

I voted for the first time today, and I've been waiting to vote for so many years that I was quite excited. Maybe I'll become a social novelist, except that I probably couldn't think of anything to say, and would never be sure it was right, at that. And I'm not irresponsible enough to be successful at it, really.

11/4/48
Life is made up of illness, convalescence, and willed relapse.

Is it perhaps that our judgment consists in comparison of different degrees of disgust?

Life moves too fast to be apprehended. Against death art is the only barrier, in that it is a recreation in sensible tempo of the components of life's fugue.

11/4/48
What the world is crying for is a popular edition of the Fuseli Obscene Drawings. Something one could hang on one's walls with real pride, that is. The details reproduced in Ruthven Todd's *Tracks in the Snow* are every bit as wonderful today as they were last year when I first read that charming book. And speaking of Fuseli, surely "Life is rapid, art is slow, occasion coy, practice fallacious, and judgment partial," says about everything. I think I'll burn the *Greek Anthology*. I'll never finish the damned thing anyway.

I wonder if one couldn't do something rather good on Christopher Smart's feeling for toads. Present it as the result of a youthful indiscretion, perhaps?

11/6/48

I received this today: "One day in June St Steven found himself on a desert road, both sides of which grew thorns and brambles. It was an exceedingly hot day and St Steven's robes clung to his body and beads of tears formed on his cheek. He walked and walked, thinking that soon there must surely be an inn on the road where he could rest and perhaps obtain some shade. His journey was long and it was only by accident that he was on this desert road.

"When he arrived at the inn he asked for water but his garb, wet and dirty, concealed his mission and his true appearance. The inn at the time was filled with herders who had come down from the hills, which from the inn were in the far horizon. They were drunk and took great amusement at St Steven's poverty and appearance. They teased him and provoked him and smilingly he tried to defend himself. But he remembered the word of God and ceased to defend himself any more. So it happened that the herders, who had recently heard of Pilate's crucifixion, tied a cross made of timbers on St Steven's back and they tied his hands so that he could not reach the cross. And they sent him on his way, warning that if he should come back on this road they would plant the cross in the ground and nail him to it.

"St Steven continued his journey with his burden and to every passing horseman he would ask for help. But none would stop and none would aid. 'My Lord,' asked St Steven, 'is this the cross that I should bear?' When it grew dark none passed and St Steven went on toward his goal, which he knew he would reach. At dawn he saw an old woman and he asked her to untie his hands, but she would have none of it. Then more and more people passed on the road but he did not see them for he knew none would help him with his cross. And so St Steven died before he reached his destination."

11/30/48

Oh my no—but you are the soul within the flower, and my heart beats still.

Everything is just fine, I tell myself, and grit my teeth until my gums bleed.

1/21/49

Walked for hours in the cold; the snow came down in large dry flakes, stinging, and crosscurrents of air intermeshed the particles, dense and comforting.

When I was a child, terrified of the dark, I would cover myself with bedclothes, and underneath the white faintly lavendered sheets would be protected from whatever horrible thing was in my room, waiting to plunge daggers into me.

The snow has grown thicker, the air colder, the wind stronger. Walked around Fresh Pond and into Watertown this afternoon full of physical well-being and joy. The wind and snow were exciting, gave spring to our stride and our faces were flushed; drank beer in a small dark-wood bar filled with men in lumber jackets, a neighborhood pub; came back in the dark and driving snow—we thought of the last of *Les Patineurs* and did entrechats and pirouettes in the wind along the Charles, completely happy; good to be [away?] from people who are embarrassed by enthusiasm. Back at school the same old depression reestablished itself, settling over me like the brown stain of the dining hall's walls. That hall full of people worrying about what anyone else is saying or thinking about them! Why should anyone stifle an impulse to be uniform? Je ne suis pas comme les autres, if I remember Rousseau, and if I am not better, at least I am different.

1/21/49

" . . . and I know now that I shall always be alone, always wandering over the earth, searching for my self in every face, pausing for instants of ecstatic recognition, then moving on . . . . ."

1/22/49

I refuse to be a slave; if life were merely a habit I should commit suicide; but even now, moreorless desperate, I cannot

108

but think, "Something wonderful may happen." It is not optimism, it is a rejection of self-pity (I hope) which leaves a loophole for life. I do not demand things. By the very token of evil there is good; it saves us from being slaves to virtue. That this is not rationalization is evident from the fact that I do not *have* to stay alive to prove that it is not a rationalization, nor on the other hand kill my self to prove the same thing. I merely choose to remain living out of respect for possibility. And possibility is the great good: it is neither cowardice nor masochism to suffer as long as one believes in possibility. We must have courage to choose and to choose the nebulous possible positive rather than the definite negative. If negation is the only definite alternative, to will is vanity. Negation is always evil; in it consists the only depravity of which the living are capable.

1/22/49

In retrospect, the saddest moment of one's life would seem to be that in which one first became aware that sensibility must be protected by intelligence if it is to survive living. It is that realization that puts the bloodshed into adolescence. And the lack of that realization makes the rest of life a bloodshed.

1/27/49

The fragility of things terrifies me! However belligerent the cactus, ash from a casual cigarette withers its bloom; the blackest puddle greys at the first drop of rain; everything fades fades changes dies when it's meddled with; if only things weren't so vulnerable! We're all children playing naked in the sun!

1/28/49

Mary McCarthy says "the most harrowing experience of man" is "the failure to feel steadily, to be able to compose a continuous pattern"; but if one does feel steadily and the pattern is horrific? If it is true that Kassner's remark about Rilke that "the conflict between judgment and feeling which is so masculine, so peculiar to men, did not exist for him," applies to me also? I suppose it is; no one can see that it is the thing that counts; I do maintain that there is no greatness divorced from being, that being is all, further, and that there is no greatness, merely the tawdry pawns of an avaricious, self-protective admiration on the part of other people, pawns, prizes to seduce the artist into imbecility, a dirty rose for the bosom of art to make it look cheap and whorish, when the whore is something else, something which sells itself for anything, for an unreckoned good or an easy satisfaction, or a place to lay its head or a pillow for tears. I feel steadily but there is no pattern, there can be no pattern, there is only being; you cannot sell yourself, you cannot stand that far apart from your self to dicker, if there is any integrity in you. There is only the giving of self and the having, the always being; you must *be* to always love and always create, the artist *is* and always loves and always creates and cannot help but love and create; I do not mean that only the artist achieves being; I am not metaphysical, quite vulgarly I mean realization of personality, but it is in the being as an entity, and in the realizing of things as entities, that one establishes being, that one lives. There is no need for a pattern if one lives, for in the realization of being one can cope with life as it comes with suffering but no bitterness.

I have not achieved being. I face sacrifice with the trembling of the coward, and suffering is deep enough and dark enough to extinguish the flame; but trembling is not defeat; I love, I create . . . . and I almost am.

APHORISM

Deceit is our own recreation of the Truth, asserts our power over matter and incidence and, like all things specific and personal, is more vivid and more valid than any abstraction, less shameful than the sterility or circumstantial defeat necessary to honesty.

[June 1949]

LAMENT AND CHASTISEMENT:
A Travelogue of War and Personality

1

What there was to say and what there was in me to say or to express just any way to get it said; what anyone and everyone had done to make them marked and separate from the rest; for they had stripped and raped us all and given us cards so we could practice our new trades newly forced in a legal way now that we were broken in and we all looked the same so nobody could tell anybody else from anybody else; everyone without an eye, the mouth a line, and a stupid soul to stare on every face I'm dead I'm dead; nothing to do but say this isn't really me because the real me slipped away just before you got here; shit I'm no dope I knew this was going to happen and I slipped away before you got here I slipped away the real me; and shit when I get the chance you'll know who the real me when I come back who I really am and you'll make no mistake you'll know it o k I won't need a number you'll know who I am.

So that for all that time everyone did nothing but act inept and wish they were somewhere else and said absolutely nothing that could tag them for something other than what they weren't by decree unless they could sneak away for a while to a library or a concert or a bar or a whorehouse.

Well, it was dull, and well, it wasn't too bad, and well, it was slow getting over with, and well, it'll never happen to ME again, and well, NOT ME NOT ME NOT ME NOT ME NEVER; and well, it wasn't so bad, and well, what the hell, and well, everyone had to do it, and well, what's the difference anyway, and well, I might as well be here as any place, and well, compared with afterward, and well, this is hell, and well, those were the good old days, and well.

2

No one had said anything to me for months and I had said nothing in return. Two young boys, cousins, who thought

I looked like someone they knew in a small town dawn
sahth because I said cuhb and pahk and they did too kept
wetting their beds at the same time to the half hour every
night and finally went back to the small town regretfully
because by that time they had changed their minds. Another
boy from the sahth had the same name as a poet of the
English Renaissance and masturbated every night in the
shower to everyone's vast amusement in that he was so stupid
anyway fit only to be a sharecropper and no one ever turned
him in for it because it was really too good fun and he got
so upset when you kidded him that it was really too good
fun to let a psychiatrist get ahold of. And from up north
there was a Greek boy who looked ten years old and could
move his hip in and out of joint when he felt like showing
off in the showers and began to have nervous seizures and
sweat and tremble and go to the hospital but the people who
knew all about queers said he was queer and just trying to
get out of it all because he had no guts they never do. There
was an older man who knew what the navy was about and
what he had to do and what everyone else had to do and saw
the big picture not just here and now but tomorrow and kept
everyone in line for the bosun because someone always wanted
to do something to someone and he always helped them if
they helped him to do something to someone he wanted to.
There was another older man who was married and loved his
wife but the war might last a long time and he was no one
to call anyone else names because to him nothing was black
and white and everything was grey and you had to be broad-
minded in this life because after all what difference did it
make how? A boy from Vermont had a love who loved him
and they had never used safes because they had never known
where to get them and he had periwinkle eyes because she
said so and she was an art student. Who looked exactly like
him except without the periwinkle eyes wrote a symphony
of chaos every night before lights out but he managed to do
everything without a bit of talent and hated Stravinsky for
being so brutal one should write like Schubert but it sounded
like Massenet or On The Plains Of Lower Pennsylvania. Oh

the arts they're all queers it's you and me joe that win the war. And the waves of course.

3

Should one allow oneself to become involved?
What is the proper spirit?
If I killed Yasuo Kuniyoshi could I sleep? Even if he told me to?
If I should die would anyone care?
Am I really me?
Is there a me to be?
Is death gratuitous?
Is suicide disinterested?
If you are there God, wiggle your ears.
I see you smiling, Mary Lou.
Did Michael Frankel or I say 'what's a guy like me doing in a place like this' first?

4

When you see the button you press it. You must determine the target by sighting along this line and squeezing like on an orange. There are several million Germans in the world and more Japanese who are utter horrors: we shall plant them, not like dragon's teeth but like Parma violets. You get right about center by listening for the mean tone, that's right sweep back and forth across the target and determine its center by your hearing, you've had musical training haven't you? I just love the Symphonie Espagnole. Milstein, of course. That's right fire. Not quite try again. And lead it just a little. That's right a little more. Now when you get an attack plan set up on this sheet you notify the officer of the deck and the communications officer but I don't know how to set it up. Someone else should have told you I can't do everyone's work who god I haven't had a liberty in days, weeks, months, I've been in the navy three thousand years without ever seeing my mother. I haven't cried so hard since 1929.

5

At Key West there is Duval Street. Except for a side street where there's a small book store with nothing but best sellers and Modern Library editions, I've never been on any street but Duval. There are bars all up and down and you drink rum or vodka, sometimes brandy-and-vodka, but the scotch is watered. They water it in Miami and then send it down. You can't get a decent scotch-and-water south of Saint Petersburg.

Everywhere there are palm trees that look like hat pins tipped with monkey fur. It's a lovely romantic place where there are soft smells and soft noises. It's terribly interesting, you know, because, you know, Ernest Hemingway has a home there. Oh my yes. If I remember it was called *Not Too Narrow Not Too Deep*. Written for Joan Crawford. Why no I haven't. All these Hollywood pinks hate Franco. And I understand he stole the whole thing from an old English short story by John Doon.

The children in Key West stay up till all hours of the night to watch the sky. The sky is nearer to the earth in Key West than anywhere else. The moon is bigger in Key West than anywhere else. Sometimes you can put your laundry out at nightfall and it will be all dry in the morning if no one steals it. There are also a number of lovely night sounds but the military police are mean.

It was in Key West that I realized I couldn't tell Haig and Haig pinch from Cutty Sark, and believe me, even though both had been watered down in Miami, it was a blow.

I also realized in Key West that if you went without lunch and dinner and drank fifteen bottles of beer the world seemed a great deal worse than it had. There is nothing like a good crying jag to make you want to hear the Brahms Concerto for Violin and Orchestra in D major, opus 77. Or is it 72. Why yes, I rather liked the Walton. Yes, Heifetz did it. Why yes, I suppose we are the only two people in the world who remember what it sounds like. No, I don't think Schoenberg is being perverse.

I saw, in a Key West barracks, the largest cockroach in the world. It was sixteen inches long and you couldn't help but respect it for it.

Except for the sky being so near, the dewy stars and the sea, I loathed Key West. Its only excuse for being there is that Wallace Stevens wrote a poem about it.

6

Choo and there is time for choo and choo and there is time; which indicates a certain surrender to the readability of certain surrender. I carried *Ulysses* with me for luck. I read it in high school because a friend who was prepping for West Point sent it to me because it was so dirty. Then I read it from the beginning and it was about something else entirely. In my locker: *Ulysses* for luck, and oh my god didn't *Portrait of the Artist as a Young Man* say everything? Should I send it to all my friends so they'd understand me? And *Swann's Way* because I liked *The Procurator of Judea* and I loved *Penguin Island.* Or was that Jules Verne? At the end of the summer there is a short period during which you should store up fuel for the coming winter. It is called *Leaves of Grass,* but don't let that fool you: it's really about sex. But why should Anatole France like Marcel Proust? It was so soothing that I almost missed the hurricane but I didn't and I went out in it and loved every minute; trees were falling down and the wind pushed and pulled and douses of water knocked things over and the sea and the sky were grey. Coconuts went boom boom boom boom and now and then squish. It was nice to think that something besides ourselves can be destructive. It was nice to think that something could be destructive and not mean it. "It's a pity," said Albert McGrail, "that the god damned barracks don't go down."

Choo and choo and out to sea, the trains still run and choo there is time for choo. For Norfolk is a cold cold city, the ass-hole of the universe, even if I did hear Grace Moore there. I'm sure she was the only good thing that had happened in Norfolk in years. The hurricane hadn't damaged Key West much at all, and Key West was heaven, with or without Wallace Stevens, compared to Norfolk. My life is a journey; whatever may happen I know that I shall never go to Norfolk again.

7

I waited at the ferry for hours and ate four apples which were sold at a candy stand by an emaciated woman. She was about fifty; her dress fell precipitously down to her waist, rushing toward the wide belt which held her skirt up. I don't know what her skirt looked like. The apples were very good. I also read two newspapers and the war news was not too good. I read a speech by President Roosevelt and one by Henry Wallace and a communique from General Douglas MacArthur. I decided that if I ever had to kill anyone I should do it for the Tennessee Valley Authority, but just then the ferry came in and people streamed around the station. My mother and father were on it; I barely recognized them and they thought I was suffering from malnutrition; all through the weekend they were not sure it was me and I was not sure it was me, but I was sure it was *them* after a few minutes, and that made it a very nice weekend. They stayed in the only decent hotel and did a very little shopping and looking while I was on duty. We had dinner each evening together, we saw a couple of shows, we did not talk about the war but about what had happened in the family and how immense my brother and sister now were, they did not come out to see the base and I did not offer to have them; it was very nice and the first thing I knew they had gone and I was in San Francisco. I now had a picture of my grand-aunt Elizabeth, who had died shortly after I left for the navy.

8

What did one do to get on or off a draft to the West Coast? Everyone who had been to sea wanted to get back and couldn't and everyone who hadn't been to sea didn't want to go and had to. Everyone went around sighing, "Well, I guess that's the navy. Yup, that's the navy for you." I was so afraid of being afraid that I didn't allow myself to think whether I could or could not get off the draft since I knew very well I couldn't. And after all I was a fairly rational person who had voluntarily enlisted in the navy and that must

mean that I had subconsciously wanted to go to sea. Think
of how much I liked Cape Cod in the summer. For one
reason: the sea. Well, then, it would all be great fun. No
matter what happened I did like the sea, and I never got
seasick unless there was too strong a smell of diesel oil.
Surely the people in charge of morale would see to it that
diesel smell was eliminated from every civilized vessel afloat.
That was that.

The train trip to San Francisco must have been unpleasant
because I remember so little about it and so much about *The
Counterfeiters*, the latter being extremely pleasant. I had
bought *The Counterfeiters* in Norfolk and read it through
practically without stopping for breath. Slightly dazed at the
end and feeling proselytic I insisted that the fellow in the
upper above me read Gide; since he had been so good as to
share a pint of rye with me the first night out of Norfolk I
felt that I should amply repay him by drawing Gide to his
attention. He reluctantly agreed to an exchange of reading
material. I got *The World, The Flesh, and Father Smith*,
which lasted me till the end of the trip; he must have liked
Gide because he never returned *The Counterfeiters*.

9

San Francisco was a welcome relief from Father Smith.
He may be a kindly pixie to everyone else, but he was a
great bore to me. I loved San Francisco. We had shore patrol
duty with eight hours on and some phenomenal time off
like twenty-four. I think Market Street is the best street in
the world of the streets in the world which I have seen.
Whenever I think of San Francisco I think of Sophie Tucker,
too, because she was at some night club while I was there
and I never could manage to afford to see her.

The first night I had liberty in San Francisco I heard the
symphony. Efrem Kurtz guest-conducted a suite arranged
for string orchestra from Corelli, Jan Smeterlin as pianist
in the Rachmaninoff Second, the Hindemith Metamorphosis
on Themes by Karl Maria von Weber, and the Tschaikovsky
Sixth. It was the first concert I had attended since a turgid

Brahms First in Norfolk and the West Coast was heaven!

In the San Francisco Art Museum there is a beautiful Van Gogh field (Auvers, I think) and some terrific Calder mobiles; and in the Civic Center at the time were still the sculptured orotund animals by someone I can't remember which were subsequently given to whatever other California city would accept them, I think Los Angeles finally did. Everything was wildly interesting.

I went down to the Arts Center in Chinatown and arranged for a practice piano; there I met some charming people who played string quartets and sang and chatted, among them a young lady who wore her black glossy hair in a large bun at the base of her skull and knew but did not care for Leonard Bernstein which I thought very snotty indeed as I was then playing his Seven Anniversaries for Piano and liking them.

The shore patrol headquarters was not far from Chinatown as I remember it, a gloomy efficient place with innumerable cages and rooms and ramps. We were just assistants waiting to go to sea so we didn't dare drink on duty in the bars we patrolled but the regulars did. When someone was brought in for drunkenness they were generally put in the main lock-up, a big room with rows of naked cots walled with wire all around; violent cases were pushed and shoved into individual cells in a cell-block near the main room; really serious offenders were kept in cells downstairs near the booking desk. The ordinary drunks in the main lock-up sank onto the cot springs toward morning or leaned against the wire sides of the enclosure shouting curses at us, the guards. I always had either a beat to walk or a station with the head of the main lock-up room. He was a pear-shaped fish-faced southerner. Like the fish, he represented Jesus Christ; he had once been a preacher he said. He was punishing people for their own good in his present employment and that was why he enjoyed it. It gave him a chance to do other people some good. He believed in punishment, it had been instituted for the well-being of human creatures by God, but he deplored the punishment of animals and loathed vivisection. At the same time one could punish men unlimitedly for drunkenness because when drunk they had lost their human dignity, and he felt that if enough punishment were meted out in this world it might very well correct everyone's behavior and thus save God all the bother on the Last Day of Judgment. He was very tolerant as to religion: he knew that every Christian must find his own way to God; the heathen might possibly have to be coerced, but it was a step to be regretted, by and large. He did not know whether he himself would coerce them or not; God had given him his understanding; he must act by the understanding God gave him, God would expect that; he would have to do what he thought right in the event of the situation ever arising; in the end he might turn out to be wrong or brutal, but God would understand that it was really His fault in giving him the understanding He had given him, and so would forgive. He had a great respect for the power of sin and sensed it acutely in people he met. Sin to him was a fever; often it would dissipate if allowed to run its course. Occasionally he helped it along by provoking the sinful to excess and then punishing them. In this way he tricked satan by calling him out into the open and dealing with him by the light of God's grace. This is not to say that he was smug or self-righteous. He admitted a mistake when and if he made one. For instance, one morning we were herding the captives down the ramp so they would be turned loose at five o'clock to return to their ships and we could go home; when I came back upstairs the head man and his burliest assistant (the latter was not God-fearing but made up for it by his efficiency, that trait indicating a subconscious sympathy with the right way to do things, namely, God's way) had pushed a negro's face into the floor; when I came in the burly one stopped twisting his arm up to his collar bone, the head man stopped kneeing him in the small of the back, and the negro was helped to his feet; he was possibly five feet tall, ninety-eight pounds, with a pipe-stem neck and head round and frail as a Christmas tree ornament; when the negro had stumbled out of hearing the head man apologized for the opinion I might be entertaining quite properly of God's guidance and correction; it was true; the negro's only offense was that he had stayed in the toilet longer than the others; the head man's judgment had been distorted by bodily fatigue and he had been wrong; he was only glad that he had erred on the side of zeal rather than laxity. He suspected innocence of dissimulation; he rather admired the courage of the frankly depraved.

When I didn't have a job in the lock-up I had a beat, usually a few streets in the bar section or the lobby of an out-of-bounds hotel or a night club. The latter were the best because sometime during the evening someone always took you out into the kitchen and fed you, and there were always people offering you drinks and delighted when you didn't accept. At that time in San Francisco the shore patrol was very lenient, if not downright pleasant; the shore patrol was there to help the enlisted man, and only hurt him if he did something wrong or proved annoying. But even then a shore patrol uniform managed to spoil almost any sailor's fun; this situation led to two kinds of shore patrolmen, the apologetic and the belligerent.

At the same time I had met charming friendly people at the Arts Center who had a string quartet and made me a steady and enraptured audience for their playing; through them I met a beautiful art student from Stanford nicknamed Natasha who wore black always and tortoise-shell combs; there was beer and Natasha loved Russian rye with anchovy paste and there was the symphony and there was the ballet and there was the fresh old city, gauche and precious, wide avenues, tiny streets, hills and troughs for cable cars, there was wind blowing, the scent of lavender, and snow in the air.

10

The sea lay all around us like lead lamé. Wrinkling, smoothing, puddling, frothing, it was not the sea I had remembered.

The waves, to George Barker when two sailors drowned, were frothy skirts; to me they were the gnashing teeth of that monstrous maw from which the flying fish and porpoise fled so hysterically and so briefly before being snapped back and ground to dull white bubbles in those metal mandibles.

This great grey tarpaulin, rent so rhythmically by inner

121

stress, is tent to what gloomy hell below the horizon?

What world is underneath, lying in death, survived only by the sea horse and the moon, that we should see floating in its sky these viscid parachutes?

The sea, the immense amoeba, groping for sustenance at all its shores, grasping the living back to its giant womb, swelling as its insatiable lust is fed, to grow, encompass, and destroy.

Someone said to me, "I am a chemist; this is just the blue I used to make things with indigo."

Later on, when the weather had grown hot, the ship smelly, the sea molten, we had to wash with salt water and special soap; there was no way of washing clothing because the ship was too crowded; the beds stank; and lying one night unable to sleep the same person said, "You know, I read a book by Henry Baudelaire once; it was given to me in college; every word was a different color like an experiment; each poem changed color from the words that were put in so you didn't know at all what the book was about and you didn't think of wondering because you knew anyway." We had a long argument that night and for the next week about Stravinsky because his wife was a musician and had told him Le Sacre du Printemps was a work of ignorance. He also recited almost perfectly part of the "Communist Manifesto" and it was good to think of it and to think of it having been written and lived by for even a short time there in the heat with every body crowded around being sweaty and smelly and snoring.

At this time I reread Ulysses, needing to throw up my sensibility and Joyce's art into the face of my surroundings; I found that Joyce was more than a match, I was reassured that what was important to me would always be important to me; deprived of music I wrote pieces which turned out to sound something like early Bartok, and I wrote awful poetry compounded of Donne, Whitman and Cummings, which I later destroyed. I found that I myself was my life: it had not occurred to me before; now I knew that the counters with which I dealt with my life were as valid in unsympathetic surroundings as they had been in sympathetic ones; for art is never a retreat; the person who cannot face himself enough to face the world on certain given terms may find that other terms are more suitable to his psyche: this is a matter of self-knowledge, not cowardice; there is no ivory tower; there are arrangements of the complex resulting from physical, intellectual, emotional, aesthetic sensitivities which dictate a particular way of life; but no one way of life is more valid than another; I had subconsciously felt this, and now I knew it. From that monstrous womb: a second birth.

11

On the horizon, up to their knees in the sea, palm trees waded sedately, walking toward us. Manus, and further beyond, New Guinea.

Where there was, so soft and red, ripe from the every afternoon rain, soil fed on purple, grey and chartreuse leaves, in the rain washed thickly down rock slopes muddled in pits of coral, quickly into dusty patches by the sun. Elephant ears all over tangled in grey roped vines with cerise flowers and plumed scatter-colored birds chattering flatteringly at monkeys heard at night in xylophone confusion on the bridge over the slow red-bubbling brook; bats swooped from flopping trees, knocked coconuts and bumped everything with a squeal of surprise like a mouse's as the sky oozed into the grey bay each night quickly when the sun went out and the flag went down. Oh how like Key West without Wallace Stevens this near sky by the surf! There were oh what charming cat's eyes on the beaches where everybody hunted swam and got ear fungus.

The ammunition dumps were situated in clearings along a broad dusty highway. Working parties went there for eight hours at a time in the hot sun; everyone blistered ached burnt and was unhappy. Outside the chapel where the Seventh Day Adventists held their meetings to convert themselves to not having insurance because the good God would take care of everything unless you insulted Him to the extent of taking care of it yourself and let us pray that everyone else will see the light it's for their own good there was a cemetery from which the corpses were being dug up, dumped out, and shovelled into transportable containers for the trip to Finchhaven. They scented our clothing and our food and our minds: the natives did the digging because no one could make a white man do that although there were few natives in the cemetery and none going to Finchhaven; only at night, when the breeze came and the clouds and shadows, and the claptrap of monkeys and chitter and rustle of birds somewhere near, did the odor's musky rot go away. It came back each morning.

Up the road from the chapel, a chapel made of strange brown wood which smelled almost as bad as the bodies, a shell had been erected for movies, USO shows, and prize fights. Around the shell, in a semicircle opposite the hill which provided natural gradation for the wooden benches facing the shell, there were courts for basketball and a field for baseball, all hard-packed, dusty and sandlot. Sunday afternoon brought everyone out either for games or the symphonic transcriptions played for people sunning on the benches in front of the shell. In explaining his *Bachianas Brasileiras* Villa-Lobos once called Bach the folk music of the universe and it is true that one afternoon in all this confusion of struggling for outlets of one kind or another amidst this stagger of recognition on every side that sanity lay only barely possible in outlets of this artificial inducement of the self to engage in something anything the Fourth *Brandenburg* Concerto established a meaning and a synthesis akin to the Elizabethan chain of being; a finger touched a button and lit up the world there all aglare with death suffering struggle defeat in motion and in blinding coherence. Not just for that moment, but vividly then, there was everything in a relationship all alive with indefinability, *da stieg ein Baum,* Orphic singing, Sartre had seen the chestnut root but Bach the world. There was for that moment again the pitch so high the light so keen spangles dancing coins flung on my shoulders and turning, rere regardant, I saw the three-masted past sailing, dark against the coast, but onward. There was, for all the zigzag, still direction. What of the rock, forgotten handkerchief, the flake of snot? the boat sailed on.

12

Hushed were the camps, hushed we all as if the faintest
sound might avalanche the world, that first day that President
Roosevelt was dead. There was no moderation, no intelligence,
no proportion, in our mourning; no man is indispensable?
every man is indispensable. And it is the illusion which great
men create that the world will not long survive them. There
is no leader but a summing up of wills: our flag at half mast
for our ideals.

That same week there was a murder. One of the negro
mess-cooks, living in their segregated hut with his radio, his
soft laugh, and his hat dyed yellow with an Atabrine tablet,
was found before their hut, his hands cut off, his testicles
tucked neatly in his cheeks, his lips sewed shut. The flag was
at half mast.

13

How can you be right if you kill everyone who is wrong?
I admire Walter Gieseking.
I admire Richard Strauss.
Does the artist do enough for humanity to obviate his
fascism?
Can you fight ideas without ideas?

BUT

Is there ever a good without evil?
Can I detach myself from Stalingrad?
Can I rationalize Franco?
Could even the greatest symphony drown out the screams
of Jews?
Is not lack of formulation progress?

14

What does one say of people? When friendship satisfies it lives
in the perfect oblivion of love; we are all sailing to Byzantium;

the artist builds a golden bird to sing on the emperor's golden
bough. So that

when we again went to sea there was Okinawa flashing red
while the natives their hair two inches above the scalp dyed
red or yellow by berry or urine bathing as they did in the
dirty surf as the palms waded slowly toward the horizon

sleeping on the open deck under the teetering mast which
stirred the stars like a finger in a porridge bowl under showers
of soot under the warm wind as the slouching like ghosts in
mist in the straits the islands like slow hippopotami passed
until there was fragrant and fruitful in doe-eyed women and
gazelle-legged men the yellow slush the Philippine rain had
slobbered

where under the rain Tagalog and Visayan tongues sang to
their bodies' waltz made music mutely hungered and ate at
street-corner cauldrons all the pimps under six years old all
the women whores all the men wistful in watching their
women in butterfly sleeves and slips promenade

(General MacArthur had returned; with him, returned
from his visit to Franco, Roxas; Osmeña was defeated shortly;
the "communist" guerrillas driven into the hills and/or shot;)

Borneo loomed nearby then gaped blue under the spatter
of what there is a midget submarine blocking the bay if
you're thinking of leaving but the ship ahead just struck a
mine and the fiss-fiss-fiss-fiss-fiss-fiss-fiss spewed feathered
fans of earth trees bones skyward in the most abstract of
designs you wouldn't get me to go ashore thank god for the
Australians everything that comes up goes down hoho right
on some Australian's head

(there is the story of the boy who wrote to his mother
before every operation that he thought he was going to die
and that he was all right after every operation as they had
planned this code but all the same she died before he did of
the strain)

swim, get tan, drink beer on that strange island where
there used to be the most beautiful women in the Pacific
but they took them all away and left only the palm trees
and put in pipes with wire-topped funnels to piss in as you

drank your beer, in and out at the same time listen to the jazz band this green stuff rots your kidneys and they've got a great big kettle underneath to catch it all and re-can it, that way it gets less green each time

(drink to me only with thine eyes and we will all the pleasures prove of Paumanok and rue de Fleurus and Clevedon Terrace and Davos-Platz and walk with Emily Dickinson and sing with Maggie Teyte and oh my how quickly the time will pass squinting back at Egon Rilke while Thomas à Kempis prays::::::::::::: there! right out there! just beyond the diving board! passed Venus the wind was blowing she was sailing along in her god damned shell!)

"it was very funny," someone said, "I mean confused when the ship actually went down although we had always known it would you know how you feel about those things it's safer always to think so because God always likes to prove you're wrong that's what the preachers mean 'no atheists in foxholes' means 'everybody's worried about their chances under fire' but then it was not so much chance the damned thing started to go down and everybody afraid to leave their GQ station and all the phones manned till all of a sudden all the stations went dead there were other ships around where the fuck were they come on wading swirling pushing don't get excited don't get excited 'back to your stations men' fuck you there was a ship alongside we were sinking pick him up and throw him to them for God's sake get those lines across Jeeseseseseseseseseseseseseseses get those lines that boom where is he there oh fuck fuck fuck where is that god damned throw those phones away you crazy fucker the ship's going down sinking get off there's the lines grab they'll pull swing on them it's deep they have to get away come on hang on and overhand over hand hand over hand overhand hand over hand hand over hand over hand hand over hand overhand hand hand hand hand hand hand where the put them below all men out of racks get them men below corpsmen corpsmen get them men below let's get out of here let's get out get that one he's weak get that one don't let go a little more mack a little more come on come on you crazy fucker come on!!!!!!!!!!!!!!! she's going down she's cut them lines cut them lines cut

(one of the last he groped hand over up the lines desperate his strength failing aching hearing as that hopeless in his ears 'cut them lines' no no wait a minute just a mo inches just a mo but the seaman in all that confusion swinging hit him smack in the skull as his arm came over the side and he fell back into the screws as the ship pulled away from the sinking)."

15

I could never recognize any plane but a Corsair because it looked like a hornet and hornets used to sting me (oh the power of memory) but I did recognize Corsairs (isn't it a pity we only remember the unpleasant?) and we screened for submarines Halsey's fuelers and when one of Halsey's screen got a kamikaze in the stack we screened Halsey and the planes struck Japan and the bomb struck Hiroshima and the war was over.

Well, the war was over.

We are fit only to be what the scum of the earth is, having received the sanction of the worm through function.

For my generation there is no hero, only the man aggregate of conflicting psychological tensions. The hero who saves his fellows is the man not strong enough to let them die; the coward is the man brave enough to let other men die when he could save them. we killed the great Japanese architect the great German scientist the great Italian musician dropped death on Hiroshima killed killed killed and yes I hate us for it killedkilledkilled

we saved our not-worth-saving world rampant with the injustice cruelty and hate which bred us;

we owe ourselves

what?

nothing?

nothing;

we are guilty?

no

guilty?

no
guilty (as the heart bleeds dawn-grey with the only killing
remorse the pain for that we could not not do)?
yes.

16

Will Mr Christopher Smart please step to the front and
center of his latter-day bedlam to lead us in prayer?

Thank you. Mr Smart appears before us today through the
courtsey of his Keeper and Maker.

The congregation will please repeat the litany:

For I am under the same accusation as my Saviour—for
they said, He sees Himself.

For I pray God for the destruction of new creatures on
this island.

For I pray God that the ostriches of Salisbury Plain, the
beavers of the Medway & silver fish of Thames may be de-
voured by disease.

For I pray to be efficient as a dog, which is best of all.

For I wish to God that desire be most High, which is my
policy.

For the tides are the life of God in the ocean, and He
sends His angel to poison the DEEP.

For He hath fixed upon the earth arches and pillars, and
the flames of hell flow under them.

For the grosser the particles the nearer the sink, & the
nearer purity the nearer degradation.

For MATTER is the lust of earth, every velleity of which
is life.

For MOTION is as the quantity of life direct, and all is
resistance.

For the Centripetal and Centrifugal forces are GOD RETAIN-
ING and REJECTING.

For the Glory of God is always in the crucifixion, but can-
not be seen for the clouds.

For the Centre is the Spirit of the hold upon the hand in
matter.

For the WEDDING GARMENTS of all men are prepared in the SUN against acceptance.

For the WEDDING GARMENTS of all women are prepared in the MOON against purification.

For there is infinite provision to kill off all the parts of Creation.

17

Let us pray:
Almighty Father, Elder-Brother, Uncle
hear Thou us;
Thou Who hath lent us this our all too brief stay in Eden
at five percent
hear us;
wait not on the cries of devils, humdrum angels, comely sprites lest Thou (oh vile impertinence) be distracted from us, Thy proper wards and servitors;
accept, O Lord
our rejection of our selves, lest it seem a barren offering before Thy altar, a vanity, a degradation of our selves;
mete, with even temper, Thy benevolent spoils, award us with Thy gratitude for adoration, and save all bitterness for the angels who are stronger or the devils who are loathesome;
O Lord
shroud, in Thy munificence, our frail spirits in Thy loving care;
soothe our sweated brows that exertion may not seem vain;
wipe, with the napkin of Thy love, our blood-stained lips, lest the victim seem pitiable and all duty guilt-ridden;
assuage with Thy balm-filled hand these nervous tremors which our exultation in Thy cause hath induced in these so temporary frames;
weep with us
O Lord
over the fatigue the arduous following of Thy divine precepts hath entailed in us, over the sorrow misery and entertainment of the world, over the snake of Thy humanity swallowing its tail;

for
O Lord
be it said not sadly of us:
we have done that which we had to do.
Amen.

EYE AT ARGOS

The walls of the city are high and dark, its bricks are petrified slime, its girders atrophied moonlight.

The sun does not dare peer through the gaps in the gate of the city.

And the albatross under the horses' hooves does not cry out as it is pummeled and sliced by the nail-fed scimitars.

The feathery white crescents of meat, washed and seasoned, are served at parties to the aborigines.

We have made this happen, looked and allowed; is it you who screams your abuse up the chimney? O brilliant night, you are waltzing above the hall of our illness! Silence their voice!

The little girl sitting by the city-gate falls face-forward in the mud.

You, poet, have addressed yourself to silence.

I ate near the center of the city, where pigeons squatted nursing the warmth of their shit until the melting snow wet their feathers. It was the time of day when the eyelids feel abrasive and your hands are like putty in your pockets. I can't remember what I had to eat because you can tell so little by daylight, I mean what a thing is, but it was very good to eat and made me feel a part of things.

There are no people in this story, you see, because there are no people. But I have seen many things happen and noticed much.

The little girl was sitting up when I walked by her, she had wiped off her face. That is, after I had eaten I walked to the city-gate again, just to look at it and to conjecture.

Beyond the gate lay the sea, thrashing against the rocks upon which the city is built. I could hear it so plainly, half out of sight, cursing my empty heart. The sea is a great curser. It never understands that I am kept here. I should cry,

O sea forgive me my being!

O sea forgive me my life!

O sea forgive me my fate!

Would the sea call back a benediction? Someone should bless us. But I have not the courage for that dialogue. That girl has found in mud what we cannot find in the stars.

The sun shines fruitfully outside the gate. Dust swims in the sun like a bower of golden fish. On the hills the grass grows rich and shaggy, the corn sags in the breeze and the wheat hums a heavy song. Rivers run across the land like fertile tears. I see that the sky is as blue as the eye within my eye. O love, can we bear to stand and look at you as a horizon?

I walked back into the darkness to which I was born. The streets swelled with buildings, throbbing windows and trembling granite blocks threatened me on every side. The stench of oil and machines was everywhere. From all sides came strangling cries. The fountains bubbled with urine and dirty towels curtained every window. Traps for mice lay unbaited on every doorstep; sweet flypaper swung in the breeze. Weak birds fell through the air to be devoured by whining tail-tight dogs. You see what it is like now, why the girl hid in the mud.

I leaned against the corner lamppost; my flesh quivered uncontrollably as the post writhed against it like a python. I must think of my strength, for without that the story cannot end. What we see, and what we know exists somewhere, even love—is only so much. I see to this point behind my cheekbone and further to my soul. The only music we have is the accidental mating of two cries. The dancers went long ago, time has washed away their posters. Our artists are born without thumbs. I am alone! I am mad!

I fell on my knees in the street scattering rats, and my hands cut on jagged stones. I felt my blood slipping onto the stones. They were so slippery I could not get up. The rats scurried quietly back, sniffing at me and sipping, nestling gently at my armpits, knees, and groin. I raised my head at a sound. A peacock with tin cans tied to its tail walked toward me slowly. Fiercely it strode toward me. I lowered my eyes. I felt its feathers. Its beak was at my ear. A great sound shattered my soul.

A STORY OUT LOUD

(Autobiography)

Something quickening, something telling everything of that. Which way did he go? Were those emeralds? How often have I cried? The spirit burgeons, the acorn nourisheth, and the vowels wax hot. On the path to the east, just sloping off before the crest of that green hill, someone hung a tree with silver ornaments like apples and earrings. And there were tiny things in the grass all along the path waving at you in a haze so delicate and wicked you could almost hear them sigh. I scratched the jade charm I always carry in my pocket with my long index fingernail and thought of good things.

Over against the other side of the hill lay a fat cloud, orange as lipstick and everything. In my pocket the fruit of the Nile valley Cleopatra used to wear around her neck. I'll be damned by an unloving Christ if I don't watch out. Pick not up trinkets, sayeth the Lord.

I sat on the book that was going to tell me. Up came a crab as big as your head and as green as everything else.

Hello.

Hello.

Something. I have something to say but the spirit just won't move me to say. There's a devil in the long grass sticking up his horns. He's an old carousing friend of mine. We walked together through a lot of bushes, good and bad, pretty and tough. Here I am talking. There's something looking over your shoulder.

It's the wind.

And you know when the spirit won't move you all the talk in the world can't make you want to talk or talk to say.

There are other troubles in the world.

I don't doubt it.

There's a lot of loving and a lot of worrying.

True.

That cloud you know is blushing.

It is. It always is. The god damned thing. There's a disease for you. A disgusting corruption of the spirit.

The crab's eyes grew red.

I think I'll read my book.

You do and I'll bite your hand off.

The tree we sat under had a deep brown trunk and wrinkles from head to foot you could put your hand in. There were wise grey spiders hanging in little sacks from the lowest branches and black ones moving higher up, arranging the leaves and biting off dead twigs. I felt as busy as a laborer. What so you say? There's no more magic outside of what you tell. Sir Gawain should come right now with all the daisies underfoot and their buttery eyes in the sunshine. I'm not going to have a legend on my hands though, I'm too young and irresponsible. There's another cloud and it's a real treat.

His eyes were black again.

You're a rude young man. Are you thinking?

I'm telling something I know.

However you say a thing is. Don't quibble. I'll get angry again, I may. Look at the horse.

Yes.

Now you're determined not to say anything, is that it? Sir. There's singing for you in the air and a brace of partridge clearly visible in that field ten miles away. How the land lies down on its back, relaxed as a dead whore, and the sun spins. I've forgotten what I wanted to say a while ago.

You know I saw you once before, in the water long ago. I was a child.

Did you have an elderly lady with you?

She had me by the hand.

Think of that. And the wind's been with you all the time and the clouds probably every other day.

Not orange clouds.

I can't change my color.

I like it. I admire it.

Well.

And all the rest. The fields and the trees and the earth underneath, always to count on. But the sun. You can never be sure of that.

Why am I told these things which I already know and the things I don't know never? Do I tell myself the same stories over and over again until I die?

No silence now. I am going to tell you to die in daylight.

The wind thrashed about the sky and my eyes whirled inward. All the trees jangled and clattered as loud as a subway. Spend your faces. Pay them out to any who ask.

Well it's something to be thought about.

I agree.

The night is a dark angel. Heaven is not ours.

Yes.

When we meet again I'll be back in the sea. Turn your eyes upon me and say farewell.

Farewell.

Something in a cave in the east and something on the prairies slow-moving as dusk. Clouds like complacent wounds, and what has the story done? All those consonants kissing and slipping away. How did all the words come into my hands for my duty and delight? I ran down the hills. I picked up stones.

There is a shape for everything. And vanishing into all are the others, their hardness and cruelty and scorn making whispers, songs and monuments. There is the surface that is meaning and the depth which the hand touches when it feels the life of stones and knows them as well as poems or words. These things we have as intimately as love or vermin and we make ourselves with them in a voyage. What the sea calls children we know. There is knowing, loving and telling to all things. And the intimacy of grey and black and white is in stones as in blind things that love, where the color springs up within the eye. How I made these patterns and spelled out these words in stones upon the shingle is the story.

The leaves swayed like a glass door and the words were birds. On the hill where I had left my book the woman was. There is telling to everything. In sun I stood and she walked in her heavy skirts with her warm flesh and she lay down to me with a song on her sweet breath.

FALSE POSITIONS

Jesus Christ, realizing that he would soon be committed to the flesh, sought an interview with Pallas Athene, she being rather an authority on human affairs among the deities, in order to brief himself on the human condition in general, and the course of action most advisable for himself in particular. But the timeless and all-knowing gods have great difficulty in communicating with each other. So vast is their area of reference (indeed, boundless!) that gods, especially if separated by ideological differences, often do not know exactly what they are talking about. This quite unnerves them, being, how shall I say it?, spirits, essences, guardians of their respective characteristics; and so they adopt for intercourse certain human characteristics, thus avoiding the conflagration which the extremity of their positions would ordinarily entail in any exchange of presences. And we must be thankful for this: it is the sole means they have of preserving the absolute nature of their qualities for our emulation and awe.

Pallas Athene, then, was annoyed at Jesus Christ. Why should I give him information, she thought, when he could easily have been gathering his own? As if I didn't know fully how little respect he and his followers have for us! Those shabby North Africans!

But her thought swerved delicately. She would inevitably change the course of his career. She giggled. Jesus Christ was even at this time an extraordinarily serious and obstinate spirit. There were those who thought that his humility was pride whole-cloth; but the gods know when something does not bear discussion, and the conjecture was never voiced off Olympus. Jesus Christ had never really thought about anyone else, and so felt that Pallas Athene must see him as he saw himself. He went toward her with the utmost confidence and a naïve joy which was based on his total lack of reflection.

So they met. Amidst the clouds neither could see the other quite clearly: Jesus was unaware of Pallas' playfulness, and she, on the other hand, did not notice how moved he was by his own sincerity. It was, after all, a large step on his part, and he could very justly be criticized for it.

Ah! Pallas said. I am ready to tell you what I can. But in my own way. I have devised a means by which you may learn a great deal about humankind, through the method as well as through the resultant information. The method is rather a dark Egyptian device, although it is thought highly of by some twentieth century Frenchmen. An IF clause and a THEN clause to answer it. But you must not know, nor I, in my turn, the IF until you know the THEN. The attempt is to plumb the subconscious, in human terms. You see, you've already learned that.

But, said Jesus, why couldn't we use a simple catechism for a model? Perhaps I should have asked Socrates . . .

My dear, she answered, he would have told you nothing but that you know nothing; and then would have smiled at his cleverness. The man is a ninny. No, a catechism would be fine if something were known, but we seek information, do we not? Believe me, humans are a mystery! I could tell you a great deal, but that way you would not learn anything you could use.

Jesus smiled humbly and winningly, but Pallas could only see him dimly and thought him rather cunning.

I shall begin with an IF, said Pallas. You must close your mind so you won't know it. Then when you have formulated a THEN I'll tell you what IF goes with it, and so on. Is that clear?

Yes.

Then let us proceed.

If only stones can be there when you need something,
    then, your majesty, I am destroyed!

Haha! said Pallas. Your turn.

If your box of animals grows too unwieldy,
    then camels ARE our dearest friends; oh dear!

If animals are puzzling to you,
    then beasts careen and quicken painfully.

That's true, said Pallas. That's the world. Now you're catching on.

If misery becomes importunate,
    then mirrors are shaped for me.

If cats are worshipped somewhere,
    then the apartment will never get painted.

Ah Egypt, said Jesus. Is that what you mean by subconscious?

Very interesting.
　　If mother missed her bus,
　　　then miracles would be extremely stuffy.
　　Touché! said Jesus, entering momentarily into the game. That's
very human, Pallas agreed.
　　If Caesar crossed the Rubicon,
　　　then I am sick at heart.
　　If insects infect your ears,
　　　then marble is made out of soap.
　　If seven giraffes were amorous,
　　　then pepper and salt could kill you.
　　If umbrellas can whirl like a skirt,
　　　then you will never learn to cook or to be really good.
　　If one of us is truly great,
　　　then one's teeth break too easily.
　　Huh! said Pallas. She thought: coward!
　　If asses are our beasts of burden,
　　　then I shall close the window and have my breakfast in bed!
　　If you tell me about stones or minnows,
　　　then there's a bigger hole in Italy then here.
　　If the Magic Flute were written by Alban Berg,
　　　then I would walk as slowly as two snails.
That's faster, you know, than just one.
Oh, said Jesus. I see
My turn, said Pallas.
　　If we were both chosen for Olympus,
　　　then uncles and aunts paid our fare to hell.
Pallas turned a red which was visible even through the mist. This
will never do, Jesus said considerately.
　　Never mind, it's your turn, snarled Pallas. Jesus trembled.
　　If the 15th of June, 1921, is Ladies-Day,
　　　then all I can say is: HORSE-SHIT!
　　I beg your pardon, said Jesus. I thought we were being human.
　　Ugh! said Pallas, and turned her shoulder away. But she felt a bit
discountenanced.
　　Jesus cleared his throat. Perhaps if I asked all the if's we might . . .
　　Pallas turned back to face him. Yes do, she said agreeably. But she
was full of rancour.

139

If minotaurs seem to frown,
then grow a bigger, better lawn and mix something on it.
Jesus decided to try another tack.
If cognition is awareness of pain,
then you'd better try stretching your eyebrows, and open up
your face in general.
Jesus winced.
If the butterfly is the nun's dragon,
then UP URUGUAY!
Pallas roared with laughter and slapped her knee.
If rocks stare openly at God,
then women will catch pneumonia.
If neon is pulled from virgins' bellies,
then your feet will get wet.
Tra la! said Pallas. Jesus became dogged.
If we do not know what magic is,
then you will wind some clock endlessly, letting the flowers
wither and die out of doors.
If you ride ten days on a subway and die,
then the marvel of it all consists in its transparency.
Jesus gathered his courage.
If twenty-one is old enough to fix everything,
then life, as a gesture, disappears.
Pallas drew herself up regally. Jesus on the other hand was furious.
If a goddess eats an avocado,
then fire is so unnecessary.
If roses are red,
then apple blossoms are angels' turds.
If you mate with snails,
then the apple is at fault.
They were going faster and faster.
If Hercules was a virgin,
then the chandelier may easily be milked.
They both laughed guiltily. Both felt quite relaxed at that.
If emeralds beat us about the head and ears,
then a bird is the next pope.
Haha! said Jesus. Delightful!

Her wit had quite won Pallas to him. She smiled graciously. Next?
If flowers can cry tears,
    then the stars really ARE shining!
Oh that's lovely! said Jesus. Isn't it? said Pallas. Oh you did wrong, she continued, not to spend more time on earth while you were waiting to become human. It does all of us good to get away from our responsibilities now and then. It's quite a garden spot, if you don't pick faults. Though I suppose you have a different view.

Well, said Jesus, getting to his feet, there's no need to go into it now. I want to thank you. It's been most edifying.

It has been fun, hasn't it? said Pallas. Goodby. She watched Jesus disappear in the mist. She sighed. I am a very nice lady, she said softly.

[A THROW OF THE DICE]

A THROW OF THE DICE NEVER Even when thrown in eternal circumstances in the midst of a wreck BE IT that the abysm whitened displays furious under an inclination a wing planing desperately its own in advance fallen again from a difficulty in gaining flight and covering the outbursts skimming the tops of bounding waves very much interiorly resumes the shadow plunged in the transparency by this alternative sail even unto adapting when extended its yawning depth inasmuch as the hulk of a ship leaning on one side or the other THE MASTER outside ancient calculations wherein the manoeuvre forgotten with age sprung forth inferring long ago he seized the bar of this conflagration at his feet of the unanimous horizon let it prepare itself let it agitate and mingle in the fist which would grasp it as one menaces a destiny and the winds the unique number which cannot be of it another mind in order to hurl it in the tempest throw back the sharp division thereof and proudly pass hesitates all unkempt corpse kept by the arm from the secret it withholds rather than as a maniac to make the play in the name of the waves one invades the chief (head) flows like a subjected beard wreck that direct the man without ship it matters not wherefore vain ancestrally to not open the clenched hand above the useless head legacy in the disappearance to someone ambiguous the ulterior immemorial demon having from null countries induced the old man towards this supreme conjunction with probability he his puerile shadow caressed and polished, rendered and washed made supple by the waves and subtracted from the lost, hard bones between the planks born of an inspiration the sea attempting by the old one or he against the sea a futile chance betrothal of which the sail of illusion sprung up again their obsession like the phantom of a gesture shall stagger totter madness SHALL NOT ABOLISH AS IF a simple insinuation of irony rolled round in all the silence or precipitated roared in some near tempest of hilarity and horror, hovers around the abysm without scattering it nor fleeing and cradles the virgin token thereof AS IF solitary forlorn feather except that a midnight toque encounters or grazes it and immobilizes in the velvet muffled by a noisy, sullen laugh this rigid whiteness derisive in opposition to the sky too much not to mark slightly whomsoever bitter prince of the derelict he caps himself as with the heroic irresistible but contained by his small virile intelligence in lightning anxious expiatory and pubescent mute laugh that IF (the lucid seigneurial plume of vertigo invisible on the forehead scintillates then shadows a tiny shadowy stature standing in its siren torsion the time to slap by impatient ultimate bifurcated scales a mystery false rock evaporated in mist which imposed a limitation to the infinite) IT WAS stellar issue NUMBER Did It Exist otherwise than scattered hallucination of agony Did It Begin And Did It Cease gushing forth when denied and shut when appearing at length by some profusion spread forth in rarity Did It Figure Itself evidence of the sum if not quite one IT SHOULD BE worse no more nor less but just as indifferently CHANCE (the pen falls rhythmic surprise of the sinister to entomb itself in the primitive foams from where long ago sprung forth their delirium to a summit tarnished in the identical neutrality of the abysm) NOTHING of the memorable crisis or it was the accomplished event in view of all void results human SHALL HAVE TAKEN PLACE an ordinary elevation pours forth the absence EXCEPT THE PLACE any inferior lapping whatsoever as if to disperse the empty act abruptly which otherwise by its falsehood would have founded the perdition in these latitudes of the vagueness wherein all reality dissolves itself EXCEPT at the altitude PERHAPS as far as a place fuses with the beyond outside of the interest shown to it in general according to such and such an obliquity by such and such a declivity of fires towards this must be the Septentrion also North A CONSTELLATION cold with forgetfulness and disuse not so much that it does not enumerate on some vacant and superior surface the successive shock siderally of a count total in formation watching doubting rolling shining and meditating before stopping at some last point which sanctifies it Every Thought Gives Forth A Throw of the Dice

[IT HAS OCCURRED TO ME TO WRITE]

It has occurred to me to write these days because things are in such a sorry state. No one knows what it is like any more, day creaks after day no more painful than the preceding, and the general sensibility is such that *Freischütz* seems as moving, or as little moving, as *Tristan*. I used to read French poetry a good deal: things upset you if you're sensitive. These days the strength of an intellectual is even forbidden to look out the window overseeing the plaza. Although we are permitted to shuffle out for bread, meat and the like, when we must.

The Bicycles of Tuonela

It's not like music, it's not like eating a whole jar of Scotch marmalade at a sitting, but there's a freshness in the air occasionally which seems to have nothing to do with the actual state of our lives or of our individual psyches. You'll find that people exclaim about it to you, perfect strangers. Though there are fewer of those now, living in such a depressed state is conducive to all sorts of familiarities both advantageous and disadvantageous, since it's always a pleasure to be said hello to, and yet you always wonder if the person is not soon going to try to borrow from your wife while you're at work, or turn up at your office when there's at last a new position and pretend to be an old friend, or, worst of worsts! hopes for a character reference.

You take your life into your hands to speak, but there's no privacy in your own home so why expect it in the streets? It's almost an imposition on people to expect them not to attempt to use you for the fulfillment of their often dire needs! And this freshness in the air, that sparkle that comes from high up! that whiff of the sea! is worth any danger, is perhaps itself the sign of danger and is worth all transgressions for the sheer nervous tonic of its excitement. We must not lose our sense of adventure simply because adventure is become too dear.

If only the darling frivolous stupid tourists with their American equipment would come back, if only one could be sure that people still got tanned on the Italian coast and travelled lavishly and spent sums of money on ice cream!

There's also a certain blue these days that even creeps into the plate glass of shop windows, not a bit subdued by the drabness of the merchandise behind it, and one thinks of going to France, or the Lowlands! next holiday, pedalling for all your worth in a throng of young people with big knees, ribbon after ribbon pushing into your eyes, shouting a snatch from *Carmen,* for once in France we may push on to the foot of the Pyrenees! da dum.

Box

The marvellously heated mornings, when you awaken sweating from the penetrating rays of old Sol, who is entirely shining everywhere and enters an enclosure entirely exterior to you, in which you languish temporally; probably you are somewhat consumed by your feverish waiting.

They are always talking about discipline, whenever anything goes wrong, like an electrical storm, like falling in love. Pretty soon there won't be any events. According to them I am an inefficient cog, Henry tells me, and for my own good he argues and for his good and for the good of the state. I know whose good. He's never even read Shakespeare. In the beginning you take any discipline that you can find useful, but as you grow, as you catch onto your own skills, zoom! you head straight into the azure. These peasants never stop writing sonnets once they start, they don't write nothing else, and they think every body else's nutty.

I tell Henry we must be as disorderly as possible, and that little enough considering our fabulous insecurity and dependence. Ah that power of words happened upon by chance! you see how clearly those words have indicated to us both the nature of our predicament, and how accurately their opposites define that message which appears written on the heart in lemon juice: human happiness, and just underneath there they are: security, independence.

"Art! think of art, Henry!" I keep saying to him. "It's more than what you say. Think of that Polish Rider who is now, even now, lengthening the shadow of twilight across the expanse of North America by means of a silence which gradually will articulate the thoroughfare of Manhattan out of existence!"

COURSE DESCRIPTION, HARVARD COLLEGE
AND
NOTES ON THE POEMS

FRANCIS RUSSELL O'HARA, A.B. 1950
COURSE DESCRIPTION, HARVARD COLLEGE

1946-47 Fall Term

English Aa — English Composition
Mr. Morrison and others

German Aa — Elementary German
Dr. Zipf and others

Music Aa — Elementary Harmony
Assistant Professor Fine

Psychology 1 — Elementary Psychology
Professor Boring

1946-47 Spring Term

English Ab — English Composition
Mr. Morrison and others

German Ab — Elementary German
Dr. Zipf and others

Music Ab — Elementary Harmony
Assistant Professor Fine

Psychology 41 — Psychology of Learning
Dr. Newman

1947-48 Fall Term

English 1a — History and Development of English Literature from the Beginning to 1700
Professor Munn

English A-1a — English Composition
Assistant Professors Schwartz and Collins

German Ca — Reading and Composition (Intermediate Course)
Assistant Professor Atkins and others

History 42a — History of England from 1688 to 1815
Dr. Elliott Perkins

1947-48 Spring Term

English A-1b	English Composition Assistant Professors Schwartz and Collins
English 1b	History and Development of English Literature from the beginning to 1700 Professor Munn
German Cb	Reading and Composition Assistant Professor Atkins and others
History 52b	The Italian Risorgimento: 1748-1870 Dr. Salvemini

1948-49

English J	English Composition Associate Professor Guérard
English 115	Chaucer Professor Whiting
English 120	English Literature from 1500 to 1603 Professor Rollins, Fall Term Assistant Professor Baker, Spring Term
English 130a	English Literature from 1603 to the Restoration Professor Murdock
English 130b	English Literature from the Restoration to 1700 Assistant Professor Wanning

1949-50

Comparative Literature 166	Forms of the Modern Novel Associate Professor Guérard
English Ga	Composition: Poetry Assistant Professor Ciardi
English 134	Drama of the Restoration and Eighteenth Century Associate Professor Baker
English 140a	English Literature from 1740 to 1798 Professor Sherburn

Comparative Literature 103	Allegory Mr. Honig
Comparative Literature 160	The Symbolist Movement Associate Professor Poggioli
English Gb	Composition: Poetry Assistant Professor Ciardi
English 182	English Critics Associate Professor Bate

NOTES TO THE POEMS

QUINTET FOR QUASIMODO

When O'Hara revised the poem he canceled section 5 and the original coda and wrote a new coda to replace it. These are the canceled stanzas:

Chorus: Dilate, my dear, my dear,
only dilation can save you.
If only the largeness of life can be felt
we may reach a happy equation

Coda
And if you can't we are doomed,
quite cheerfully, love, my love,
quite cheerfully, cheerfully doomed, my love,
doomed, doomed, doomed.

HOMAGE TO JOHN WEBSTER

An earlier title was: Duodecad

DIRGE

Earlier titles were: I Sorrow, I Analyze
Marian's Mortality, a Dirge

FOR NATASHA

An earlier title was: To Djuna

[WHITE AND CASUAL HOW THE BREATH]

Written for John Ciardi's course at Harvard; he gave it an A.

PORTRAIT OF JAMES JOYCE

MS 660 has an earlier canceled title: fantasia on a theme by joyce

PORTRAIT OF J CHARLES KIEFE

Like PORTRAIT OF JAMES JOYCE this poem seems to imitate the closed up punctuation affected by José Garcia Villa, a Philippine poet of the period.

MORGENMUSIK

MS 650 line 21 originally read: "Life's only suitable accompaniment." The last two words were changed to "sure attainment." and alongside O'Hara wrote: (entertainment?)

A SENTENCE

MS 648 has these canceled lines 2 and 3:

> where mermaids still
> thrash, cavort and whistle

[IT SNOWS BEHIND MY EYES]

From a letter to Kenneth Koch.

AT THE SOURCE

Ben Weber's MS supplies the place and date of composition.

TO LOVER, TO GOD

MS 639 presents this poem rather artfully: The words of the first stanza have been typed on 12 sheets of paper so that each word is visible through a hole in the preceding sheet. The second stanza is a collage of words typed on white paper, cut out, and pasted on purple construction paper in two arching lines.

LISTEN, MY ENEMIES . . . .

O'Hara credited this title to Alex Comfort.

PASTORALS

When O'Hara edited "Oranges: 12 Pastorals" for publication, he omitted these seven "Pastorals." In MS 296 they were originally numbers 2-4, 11-13, and 15. (The twelve "Oranges" were originally numbers 1, 5-10, 14, and 16-19.)

NEW YORK

MS 666 has these canceled last lines:

> the flames roar, the fire goes out,
> embers kiss a charred snout.

A SUITE OF VOWELS (the two "Popular Songs"); AT THE THEATRE; FIRST NIGHT; AT THE SOURCE; THE MAN WITHOUT A COUNTRY; VARIATIONS ON A THEME BY SHELLEY; TRAVEL; AMERICA: A LITANY

These poems were included in "A Byzantine Place," O'Hara's Hopwood award thesis.

THE MAN WITHOUT A COUNTRY

Identified as about Ed Hale and dated Cambridge, October 1949, in Ben Weber's MS.

PRINCESS ELIZABETH OF BOHEMIA, AS PERDITA

In MS 587 the "Ed" of line 8 is identified as Ed Hale.

[IN PERIL OF MY LIFE AT THE HANDS]

Maureen Granville-Smith's conjectural transcription of a poem written on the inside of an envelope postmarked May 29, 1950. The poem appears to have been addressed to Violet Lang.

INDEX OF TITLES AND FIRST LINES

Titles of poems are given in italic type

GREY FOX PRESS BOOKS

Allen Ginsberg: *The Gates of Wrath: Rhymed Poems* 1948-1952
Gay Sunshine Interview (with Allen Young)

Frank O'Hara: *Early Writing*
Poems Retrieved
Standing Still and Walking in New York

Charles Olson: *The Fiery Hunt & Other Plays*

Gary Snyder,
Lew Welch &
Philip Whalen: *On Bread & Poetry*

Lew Welch: *How I Work as a Poet & Other Essays/Plays/Stories*
I, Leo — An Unfinished Novel
Ring of Bone: Collected Poems 1950-1971
Selected Poems
Trip Trap (with Jack Kerouac & Albert Saijo)

Philip Whalen: *Decompressions: Selected Poems*
Off the Wall: Interviews with Philip Whalen
Scenes of Life at the Capital